COMPREHENSIVE RESEARCH
AND STUDY GUIDE

Samuel T. Coleridge

EDITED AND WITH AN INTRODUCTION
BY HAROLD BLOOM

BLOOM'S MAJOR
SHORT STORY
WRITERS

Anton Chekhov

Joseph Conrad

Stephen Crane

William Faulkner

F. Scott Fitzgerald

Nathaniel Hawthorne

Ernest Hemingway

O. Henry

Shirley Jackson

Henry James

James Joyce

D. H. Lawrence

Jack London

Herman Melville

Flannery O'Connor

Edgar Allan Poe

Katherine Anne Porter

J. D. Salinger

John Steinbeck

Mark Twain

John Updike

Eudora Welty

BLOOM'S MAJOR
WORLD POETS

Maya Angelou

Robert Browning

Geoffrey Chaucer

Samuel T. Coleridge

Dante

Emily Dickinson

John Donne

T. S. Eliot

Robert Frost

Homer

Langston Hughes

John Keats

John Milton

Sylvia Plath

Edgar Allan Poe

Poets of World War I

Shakespeare's Poems
& Sonnets

Percy Shelley

Alfred, Lord Tennyson

Walt Whitman

William Wordsworth

William Butler Yeats

Samuel T. Coleridge

BLOOM'S

MAJOR

POETS

EDITED AND WITH AN INTRODUCTION
BY HAROLD BLOOM

© 2001 by Chelsea House Publishers, a subsidiary of
Haights Cross Communications.

Introduction © 2001 by Harold Bloom.

Printed and bound in the United States of America.

First Printing
1 3 5 7 9 8 6 4 2

Library of Congress Cataloging-in-Publication Data
Samuel Taylor Coleridge / edited by Harold Bloom
       p. cm. — (Bloom's major poets)
    Includes bibliographical references and index.
    ISBN 0-7910-5933-2 (alk. paper)
    1. Coleridge, Samuel Taylor, 1772–1834—Criticism and
interpretation. I. Bloom, Harold. II. Series.
PR4484.S26   2000
823'.7—dc21   00-055588
                                    CIP

Chelsea House Publishers
1974 Sproul Road, Suite 400
Broomall, PA 19008-0914

The Chelsea House World Wide Web address is
http://www.chelseahouse.com

Contributing Editor: Janyce Marson

Produced by: Robert Gerson Publisher's Services, Santa Barbara, CA

Contents

User's Guide

This volume is designed to present biographical, critical, and bibliographical information on the author's best-known or most important poems. Following Harold Bloom's editor's note and introduction is a detailed biography of the author, discussing major life events and important literary accomplishments. A thematic and structural analysis of each poem follows, tracing significant themes, patterns, and motifs in the work.

A selection of critical extracts, derived from previously published material from leading critics, analyzes aspects of each poem. The extracts consist of statements from the author, if available, early reviews of the work, and later evaluations up to the present. A bibliography of the author's writings (including a complete list of all books written, cowritten, edited, and translated), a list of additional books and articles on the author and the work, and an index of themes and ideas in the author's writings conclude the volume.

~

Harold Bloom is Sterling Professor of the Humanities at Yale University and Henry W. and Albert A. Berg Professor of English at the New York University Graduate School. He is the author of over 20 books, including *Shelley's Mythmaking* (1959), *The Visionary Company* (1961), *Blake's Apocalypse* (1963), *Yeats* (1970), *A Map of Misreading* (1975), *Kabbalah and Criticism* (1975), *Agon: Toward a Theory of Revisionism* (1982), *The American Religion* (1992), *The Western Canon* (1994), and *Omens of Millennium: The Gnosis of Angels, Dreams, and Resurrection* (1996). *The Anxiety of Influence* (1973) sets forth Professor Bloom's provocative theory of the literary relationships between the great writers and their predecessors. His most recent books include *Shakespeare: The Invention of the Human*, a 1998 National Book Award finalist, and *How to Read and Why*, which was published in 2000.

Professor Bloom earned his Ph.D. from Yale University in 1955 and has served on the Yale faculty since then. He is a 1985 MacArthur Foundation Award recipient, served as the Charles Eliot Norton Professor of Poetry at Harvard University in 1987–88, and has received honorary degrees from the universities of Rome and Bologna. In 1999, Professor Bloom received the prestigious American Academy of Arts and Letters Gold Medal for Criticism.

Currently, Harold Bloom is the editor of numerous Chelsea House volumes of literary criticism, including the series BLOOM'S NOTES, BLOOM'S MAJOR DRAMATISTS, BLOOM'S MAJOR NOVELISTS, MAJOR LITERARY CHARACTERS, MODERN CRITICAL VIEWS, MODERN CRITICAL INTERPRETATIONS, and WOMEN WRITERS OF ENGLISH AND THEIR WORKS.

Editor's Note

My Introduction centers upon "Kubla Khan" and "The Rime of the Ancient Mariner," stressing Coleridge's fears about his own creative powers.

Of the more than two dozen Critical Views, I find particularly useful Morse Peckham on "The Ancient Mariner," and Paul Magnuson on "Frost at Midnight."

I commend also Rosemary Ashton on "Christabel" and Reeve Parker on "Dejection: An Ode."

"Kubla Khan" is illuminated by David Perkins and by Kathleen Wheeler. But all of the excerpts, on all five poems, offer distinguished insights.

Introduction

HAROLD BLOOM

Coleridge had the dark fortune of being eclipsed by his best friend, William Wordsworth. What we think of as modern poetry is Wordsworthianism, the evanescence of any poetic subject except for the poet's own subjectivity. Two years younger than Wordsworth, Coleridge actually invented what was to be the Wordsworthian mode in such early poems as "The Eolian Harp" (1795) and "Frost at Midnight" (1798), the immediate precursors of Wordsworth's "Tintern Abbey" (written later in 1798). But Coleridge had an almost Kafkan sense of guilt and of self-abnegation. He became Wordsworth's follower, enhancing their joint volume, *Lyrical Ballads* (1798) with his magnificent *The Rime of the Ancient Mariner*. Since the two parts of *Christabel* were composed in 1798 and 1800, "Kubla Khan" around 1798, and "Dejection: An Ode" in 1802, Coleridge's crucial poetic achievement is pretty much the work of four years, and essentially ended when he was 30. When one considers how unique and original Coleridge's poetic endowment was, it is a great sorrow that only a few fragments attest to his gift after 1802.

Perhaps Coleridge's greatest achievement, like Emerson's after him, was in his notebooks, which afford an extraordinary image of his complex and restless mind. Yet, for the common reader, Coleridge is no longer the Sage of Highgate, but the author of a few absolute poems, "Kubla Khan," and *The Rime of the Ancient Mariner* in particular. Coleridge had projected an epic on the fall of Jerusalem to the Romans (A.D. 70), and rather wonderfully "Kubla Khan" somehow issued from that outrageous ambition. No reader could know this from chanting the gorgeous fragment, which should be memorized and indeed recited aloud. But this foreground helps explain the sense of "holy dread" in "Kubla Khan," and its general atmosphere of potential profanation.

The hidden theme of "Kubla Khan" appears to be Coleridge's fear of his own genius, his own daemonic powers. The poem's genre is what William Collins, following John Milton, established in his "Ode on the Incarnation of the Poetical Character." There a new Apollo, a "rich-haired youth of morn," is manifested in the guise of the post-Miltonic, pre-Romantic Bard of Sensibility, a direct ancestor of

William Blake as well as of Coleridge. "Kubla Khan" concludes with a vision of a youth with flashing eyes and floating hair, who has found his way back to an unfallen existence, where he has drunk "the milk of Paradise." This youth is the poet that Coleridge both longed and feared to become, the celebrant of a new imaginative power, one that would repair the fall not only of Jerusalem but of Man.

The Rime of the Ancient Mariner, so frequently interpreted as a Christian parable of the Fall of Man, instead is a phantasmagoria of the unlived life, one so compulsive that the poem never will know (nor can we) why gratuitous crimes and gratuitous releases should take place. Whereas the Christian Fall results from an act of disobedience, the Ancient Mariner simply *acts,* without willing and yet with terrible consequences. As I read this great ballad, it is a poem of the Imagination's revenge upon those who live in a world without Imagination. Coleridge rightly said that it had no true moral, and indeed should have had no moral at all. Instead, it offers a visionary cosmos as compelling as that in Kafka's stories and parables. Coleridge, like Kafka, makes his work uninterpretable, but in turn the matter for interpretation becomes just that movement away from interpretability. Kafka gives us a New Kabbalah, and so does Coleridge. The cosmos of *The Rime of the Ancient Mariner* is not sacramental but Gnostic; the divinity is estranged or hidden, and we find ourselves in the emptiness the ancient Gnostics called the Kenoma. There we wander, there we weep, unless we suffer the ultimate, compulsive fate of the Ancient Mariner, who ends as a haunter of wedding feasts, always retelling his own story, in a kind of parody of ecological wisdom.

We can surmise that the two extreme figures of Coleridge's bipolar vision are the youth of "Kubla Khan" and the Ancient Mariner. Perhaps they are caught in a perpetual cycle together, in which at last the newly incarnated Poetic character must age into a fundamentalist of what Coleridge called the Primary Imagination. That is "primary" only in being initial; otherwise it is repetition, unlike the secondary or higher imagination that has drunk the milk of Paradise, with consequences immediately ecstatic but finally catastrophic. ❈

Biography of Samuel Taylor Coleridge

Samuel Taylor Coleridge was born in 1772. His father, the Reverend John Coleridge, was a distinguished classical and Hebrew scholar who held the prestigious position of headmaster of the King's School at Ottery St. Mary. By all accounts his mother, Ann Bowdon Coleridge, was cold, detached, and ambitious. In Coleridge's accounts of childhood, he scarcely mentions his mother, though in his poetry he writes poignantly and movingly about young children, especially of the infant's need for a mother's love. Coleridge did, however, identify strongly and lovingly with his eccentric father, a man who has been described as scholarly and absent-minded, oblivious of his dress and appearance. As an adult, Coleridge adopted many of his father's characteristics; those who knew Coleridge remarked that his own slovenly appearance was in sharp contrast to his brilliance and eloquence.

As a young boy, Coleridge was dreamy and precocious; he was an avid reader from a very early age. In an October 1797 letter, Coleridge told Thomas Poole, "[I] read every book that came in my way without distinction." He was also very lonely; perhaps his books served to keep him company.

When Coleridge's father died in 1781, the youth moved into a much smaller house with his mother and sister. Shortly thereafter, a friend of Coleridge's father, Judge Buller, arranged for the young man to enter Christ's Hospital school, a famous boarding school in London where the sons of poor gentry received an excellent preparatory education. Coleridge began his studies there in September 1782. One of Coleridge's schoolmates at Christ's Hospital was Charles Lamb, who would go on to a career as an essayist and critic; Coleridge and Lamb became lifelong friends.

Toward the end of his term at Christ's Hospital school, Coleridge began to take an interest in political affairs. The French Revolution had taken place in 1789, and like many other students, he was enthusiastic about the promise of social and political revolution in France. Replacing that country's monarchy, Coleridge felt, would bring about reforms and social equality. He anticipated a republican system of government, in which leaders are elected by citizens, all of whom have an equal say, as a far better form of government than the monarchy.

In the fall of 1791 Coleridge entered Cambridge University, which at the time was the academic center of reform activity in England. Within the academic environment, Coleridge's views became increasingly radical. One of his most influential friends was William Frend, a fellow student who left the Church of England and declared himself to be Unitarian, a Protestant sect not recognized in England. When Frend stood trial for publishing a pamphlet advocating freedom for religious dissenters to hold government jobs, Coleridge was one of the noisy students seated in the gallery in his support. Their presence accomplished little, however; Frend was found guilty and expelled from Cambridge.

For Coleridge, the Cambridge years were also a time of dissolution and financial hardship. He began visiting prostitutes, drinking heavily, and taking opium. These habits led to tremendous debts. In 1793, in an act of desperation, Coleridge enlisted in a military regiment under the name Silas Tomkyn Comberbache. He joined His Majesty's Fifteenth Light Dragoons, so that he would have food and a place to stay, but he proved to be a very poor horseman. As a result, his military service consisted mostly of nursing a fellow soldier with smallpox and writing letters to the wives and sweethearts of other soldiers. His time in the Light Dragoons was brief; Coleridge's brother James and his friends Charles Valentine LeGrice and Robert Allen intervened to help him get out of the military. Though at first the army insisted on finding a substitute before they would discharge Coleridge, eventually Coleridge's commanding officer accepted his plea of insanity.

Although Coleridge returned to Cambridge, he left in 1794 without a degree. Around this time, he met the poet Robert Southey, a fellow radical who would have an enormous influence on Coleridge. Together, the two young men planned to establish a utopian democratic community in America, which would be governed by what Coleridge termed "Pantisocracy"—equal rule by all. An American real-estate agent convinced them to locate their proposed community along the banks of the Susquehanna River in Pennsylvania. Coleridge's commitment to this plan was great enough for him to marry Sara Fricker (the sister of Southey's financier), but the community never materialized.

Though Coleridge and Sara were not well-matched, their marriage was at first a happy one, despite their financial troubles. In 1796, a year after the marriage, Coleridge published a political magazine, *The Watchman*, but it folded after just 10 issues. Coleridge was rescued from debt by Thomas and Josiah Wedgwood, the sons of the famous pottery's founder. They granted Coleridge an annuity of 150 pounds so he could pursue his literary career.

Coleridge had met the poet William Wordsworth in 1795, and in 1797 the Coleridges moved to Nether Stowey in England's Lake District to be near Wordsworth and his sister Dorothy. This move initiated a period of close communication and poetic collaboration between the two poets that culminated in their volume of poetry, *Lyrical Ballads*, published in 1798. *Lyrical Ballads* was the first important English publication of what came to be termed "romantic" poetry. Coleridge's major contribution was his long poem, "The Rime of the Ancient Mariner." He also wrote the poem "Frost at Midnight," as well as the fragment "Kubla Khan," around this time; the latter is considered one of his most enduring poetic achievements, although it would not be published for nearly 20 years. The first part of *Christabel* was also written in 1798.

After the publication of *Lyrical Ballads*, Coleridge toured Germany and studied at Göttingen University, beginning a lifetime study of German philosophers such as Immanuel Kant. As a result, he rethought his position on philosophy, religion, and literature.

When he returned to England in 1799, Coleridge's marriage was failing. His romantic attention focused now on Sara Hutchinson, whose sister Mary would later become William Wordsworth's wife. By 1802, the year in which Coleridge's daughter Sara was born, he was estranged from his wife and spent very little time at home. His health was declining as well, thanks to the cool, damp climate of the Lake District, and he took opium to relieve his symptoms. This led to addiction.

The second edition of *Lyrical Ballads* was published in 1800; this edition contained a preface by Wordsworth that explained his theory of poetry. The preface to *Lyrical Ballads* would become a guide to other Romantic poets of the early 19th century. Coleridge, meanwhile, wrote the second part of *Christabel* in 1800 and wrote "Dejection: An Ode" in 1802.

Coleridge embarked on a walking tour of Scotland with William and Dorothy Wordsworth in August 1803. The tour was not a success, and Coleridge separated from the others and pursued the tour alone. This resulted in a cooled relationship between the two poets. In 1804, shortly after his return from Scotland, Coleridge set out for the Mediterranean island of Malta, hoping to restore his health.

The six-week trip to Malta was a difficult one, and Coleridge suffered bouts of seasickness. When he arrived at last, he prayed for spiritual and physical aid; however, the notebooks he kept in Malta indicate he was able to shake neither his physical illness nor his opium habit during the time he was there. The notebooks also document a period of painful self-analysis. He returned home before Christmas 1806 a broken man—hopelessly addicted to opium, subject to horrifying nightmares, and permanently estranged from his wife.

Coleridge wrote little poetry after 1802; instead, he established himself as one of England's foremost literary critics. Between 1808 and 1819, Coleridge gave seven series of brilliant lectures on Shakespeare; he included most of these in his *Biographica Literaria* (1817), an important two-volume collection of critical essays.

His opium addiction continued unchecked; in 1816 Coleridge confessed to Byron his daily habit of swallowing enormous doses of the drug. Finally, he took up residence with a London doctor, James Gillman, so that his opium consumption could be medically supervised. By all accounts, Dr. Gillman was a patient and kindly man; during his stay with the Gillman family, Coleridge finally found happiness and tranquility. He remained with them for the rest of his life.

In his last years, Coleridge was entirely absorbed in studying philosophy and religion. When he died in 1834, he had finally achieved peace of mind and had reconciled with both his wife and the Wordsworths. The brilliant poet-critic will forever be remembered as a man of powerful imaginative vision. ❀

Thematic Analysis of
"The Rime of the Ancient Mariner"

Written in 1797 and first published in 1798, "The Rime of the Ancient Mariner" has been interpreted as both a tale of the supernatural, in the Gothic tradition of superstition, magic spells, gloomy atmosphere, and treacherous journeys, and a religious allegory, a morality story embedded within the tale of the Mariner's fate after killing a divine bird. However, the circumstances behind the creation of this fantastic tale were actually quite mundane; one of Coleridge's primary motivations for writing the poem was to raise money for a walking tour that had already begun.

On November 13, 1797, Coleridge and Wordsworth (and Wordsworth's sister, Dorothy) had set out from Alfoxden, headed toward Watchet, a quaint old port not far from Bristol. As the evening drew on, Coleridge and Wordsworth began to plan a way to defer the costs of the tour they had already embarked upon; they decided to write a Gothic ballad, a type of poetry Coleridge remembered from his childhood. Gothic ballads were short yet highly dramatic poems that originated in the oral folk tradition, and they were much in vogue during the 1790s. Coleridge and Wordsworth planned to publish their creation in the *Monthly Magazine*. As a result, Coleridge created "The Rime of the Ancient Mariner." When finished, it proved to be far more complex than the Gothic tradition which so heavily influenced it; what's more, it was also a "modern" revision of the medieval allegory to which it bears striking resemblance.

"The Rime of the Ancient Mariner" is Coleridge's retelling of a strange dream of John Cruikshank, one of his neighbors in Nether Stowey. Cruikshank dreamed of a skeleton ship, and Coleridge embellished the dream to include the mortal sin of an old navigator, the punishment that ensued, and the navigator's eventual atonement for his sinful act. Although the poem was originally planned as a joint literary effort by Wordsworth and Coleridge (and it was eventually included in their collaborative work, the *Lyrical Ballads*, first published in 1798), the poem is essentially Coleridge's. A few details, however, are attributed to William Wordsworth, such as the ship navigated by the dead sailors who surround the Mariner. Wordsworth also contributed one of the poem's central events, the haunting of a ship's officer who had shot an albatross. (Wordsworth had happened across this detail in Captain George Shelvocke's *Voyage Round the World by the Way of the Great South Sea* [1726].)

Part 1 of "The Ancient Mariner" introduces many of the themes that are explored throughout the poem. In the first stanza an ancient Mariner with "a long gray beard and glittering eye" intrudes upon a wedding guest and prevents him from joining the marriage celebration. In his detention of the guest, the old Mariner is interfering with one of the sacraments, a formal religious act attesting to one's faith and adherence to the teachings of the Catholic Church. Furthermore, there are three wedding guests, but only one is stopped, and though he asks, "Now wherefore stopp'st thou me?" neither he nor the reader is ever told why. We can only surmise that this frail old sailor with his "skinny hand" and "glittering eye" has either some supernatural, hypnotic effect (known as mesmerism in Coleridge's time) or that he functions as a spiritual messenger whose powers are beyond mortal explanation. "He holds him with his glittering eye— / The Wedding-Guest stood still, / And listens like a three years' child: / The Mariner hath his will." And though we are told that "the ship was cheered" and that the bride is "[r]ed as a rose," the atmosphere on deck becomes increasingly sinister. The Mariner is absolutely intent on describing the dire events that lead to his terrible punishment, and the Wedding-Guest "cannot choose but hear."

By the end of Part 1 the sacred nature of the albatross is established, "[a]s if it had been a Christian soul." The bird also participates in religious devotions; for instance it observes the canonical hours, as "it perched for vespers nine." But the Mariner's profane impulses kill this sacred messenger, and by giving in to those impulses, the Mariner violates a social code (prevalent in medieval literature) that required a benign stranger be offered hospitality and warm welcome. (The albatross, though unfamiliar with the customs of the ship, "ate the food it ne'er had eat," dutifully returned every day, despite "mist or cloud, on mast or shroud.")

In **Part 2**, we get a detailed description of the landscape and the climate of the Mariner's imagination after he killed the sacred bird. The sea is gloomy and difficult to navigate, "[s]till hid in mist," and though "the good south wind still blew behind," moving the ship to an undisclosed destination, our sense of foreboding grows as we read "no sweet bird did follow." The other sailors become like the chorus in a Greek tragedy, commenting on the Mariner's guilty conscience. "For all averred, I had killed the bird / That made the breeze to blow."

In the absence of the sacred bird, the environment, as described by the Mariner, becomes a vision of hell, with the inversion of the natural phenomena, "[t]he bloody Sun, at noon," and a retrogression to a prehistoric time where "slimy things did crawl with legs / Upon the slimy sea." The ship is left with only the tormenting memory of the sustenance the sea had once provided; while still alive, the Mariner experiences the state of death, where everything is devoid of motion and vitality. One of the most memorable images of this life-in-death is the often quoted description of a paralyzed ocean: "Day after day, day after day, / We stick, nor breath nor motion; / As idle as a painted ship / Upon a painted ocean." The oppressive background gives way to superstition, including a reference to St. Elmo's fire, an atmospheric electricity seen on a ship's mast and believed by some to predict disaster. "About, about, in reel and rout / the death-fires danced at night."

In **Part 3**, the sense of deprivation intensifies as the senses are assaulted and basic human needs are denied. Time itself seems merciless and tyrannical, offering neither hope nor end to the suffering. "There passed a weary time. Each throat / Was parched, and glazed each eye. / A weary time! A weary time!" The images of hell accelerate and increase as do the nightmarish visions of preternatural spirits that cannot be seen but nevertheless wreak untold violence for the killing of the sacred albatross. Coleridge builds a "poetic" collaboration between a distorted natural world and a vengeance-seeking spiritual world. "With throats unslaked, with black lips baked, / We could nor laugh nor wail; / Through utter drought all dumb we stood." Further on, the avenging spirits assume a frightening materiality as Death makes herself known: "Are those *her* ribs through which the Sun / Did peer, as through a grate? / and is that Woman all her crew? . . . Is DEATH that woman's mate? . . . The Night-mare LIFE-IN-DEATH was she." Death has won the game with the mariners and her fearful price is that all the sailors must die, "[f]our times fifty living men, (And I heard nor sigh nor groan) . . . They dropped down one by one," leaving the Mariner completely alone and isolated.

Part 4 brings us back to the detained Wedding-Guest who has been paralyzed by the frail but powerful old sailor. The Mariner exercises absolute emotional and physical control over the unwilling guest, who says, "'I fear thee, ancient Mariner! / I fear thy skinny hand!'" The Mariner addresses the Wedding-Guest's terrible anxiety with a subtle, yet-unexplained response: all will somehow turn out well in the end because he, the Mariner, is still alive. "Fear not, fear not, thou Wedding-Guest! / This body dropped not down." The Mariner continues with his tale of how he, the sole survivor of a mortal sin brought on by his own hand, lived through his hell on earth while surrounded by death and destruction. "The many men, so beautiful! / And they all dead did lie: / And a thousand thousand slimy things / Lived on; and so did I."

Something crucial happens at the end of this section; the Mariner begins to undergo a spiritual rebirth, signaled by a transformation in his understanding of the terrors he has been forced to endure. While watching the snakes and other creatures beyond the shadow of the ship, where light and vision are possible, the Mariner reflects how joyful these creatures seem in their celebration of life. "O happy living things! no tongue / Their beauty might declare / A spring of love gushed from my heart, / And I blessed them unaware." Though he is not yet conscious of his own spiritual awakening, his expression of love begins his journey toward the expiation of sin and eventual salvation. (This same spiritual awakening, as we will see, is completely absent in "Christabel.")

Part 5 continues the process of spiritual renewal. The Mariner becomes less conscious of his own physical, material being as he begins to see his own soul. At one point, he says he has lost all sensation; he moves without feeling, another life-in-death experience: "I moved, and could not feel my limbs: / I was so light." The experience intensifies as Nature participates by demonstrating a frenetic energy: "The upper air burst into life! . . . And to and fro, and in and out, / The wan stars danced between." This motion inexplicably does not move the ship, and yet it propels it nevertheless. In a similar fashion, the dead sailors on deck begin to groan without speaking as they move their lifeless limbs, becoming animated corpses. "They groaned, they stirred, they all uprose; / Nor spake, nor moved their eyes; / It had been strange, even in a dream, / To have seen those dead men rise." The dead sailors assume their former functions on board the ship, "a ghastly crew."

This weird description makes the Wedding Guest anxious, and he interrupts the Mariner. The Mariner assures him that the quasi-resurrected crew do not return in pain and anguish—only their souls have returned and they are "[b]ut a troop of spirits blest," now able to sing heavenly songs rather than the common language of mortal man. "And now 'twas like all instruments, / Now like a lonely flute; / And now it is an angel's song, / That makes the heavens be mute." Coleridge's imagery of the animated corpse is not simply a supernatural element but, rather, reflects the poet's interest in the scientific and pseudo-scientific issues of the late 18th century. He was influenced by the work on electricity and magnetism of Joseph Priestley, a scientist and radical reformer who shared many of the same political beliefs with the young poet.

A little further on, when the Mariner falls into a swoon, yet another version of a life-in-death experience, he hears two voices in the air speaking to one another, wondering if he is the one who "laid full low / The harmless Albatross." Once the voices have correctly identified the Mariner, they agree that though he has already paid for his terrible crime, he needs to expiate his sin more fully. "The man hath penance done, / And penance more will do."

Part 6 continues with the Mariner still under a spell, having fallen down by some invisible power that causes him to jerk back and forth. His condition resembles a religious trance, a state where one forgets the body and is instead transported into a spiritual realm. Meanwhile, the dialogue between the two voices continues. The first voice inquires about the strange force that mysteriously moves the ship, to which the second voice responds that it is propelled from beneath, then quickly advises the first spirit to move quickly before the Mariner awakens. "Fly, brother, fly! more high, more high! . . . For slow and slow that ship will go, / When the Mariner's trance is abated."

When the Mariner awakens, he is confronted with the sight of the dead men, gathered together in a collective stare from which he cannot turn away. The sight is but a spell and quickly vanishes, leaving the Mariner fearful of the next vision he may be compelled to witness. "Like one, that on a lonesome road / Doth in fear and dread . . . Because he knows, a frightful fiend / Doth close behind him tread."

However, his fear is soon transformed into joy; that change is signaled by the wind, which for the romantic poets always meant spirit. The wind is a benign and healing presence: "It raised my hair, it fanned my cheek / Like a meadow-gale of spring." That healing presence continues to manifest itself as the Mariner becomes aware of celestial beings, the highest ranking angels in heaven, on board the ship. "The seraph band, each waved his hand: / It was a heavenly sight." This is a holy presence, the vision of which no mortal being has the power to remove. "Dear Lord in Heaven! it was a joy / The dead men could not blast." The Mariner, having confessed his sin and endured his penance, has finally been granted absolution by a third presence, a good Hermit. "He'll shrieve my soul, he'll wash away / The Albatross's blood."

In the concluding section, **Part 7**, the Mariner, accompanied by the Hermit, is miraculously saved from drowning as the ship suddenly sinks. "Stunned by that loud and dreadful sound, / . . . Like one that hath been seven days drowned / My body lay afloat." Shortly thereafter, the Mariner "stood on the firm land," and he immediately asks the Hermit to hear his confession. "O shrieve me, shrieve me, holy man." When asked by the Hermit to state what type of man he really is, his body is subjected to a violent twisting by an invisible force; this overwhelming physical gesture causes him to speak up. As a result, the Mariner is at last set free. "Forthwith this frame of mine was wrenched / With a woeful agony, / And then it left me free."

An evil spirit leaves his body. This last "trial" in the Mariner's imaginative journey signals his final step toward spiritual redemption. The completion of the redemptive process has a strange effect on the Mariner, who is now compelled to tell his tale to a stranger whenever the right one appears. "I have strange power of speech; / That moment that his face I see, / I know the man that must hear me."

And so the poem of the ancient Mariner ends with the Wedding-Guest unable to attend the marriage because he is "stunned, /And is of sense forlorn." Though the tale is over, and the Mariner has learned the lesson that man must love "all things both great and small," the end of the narrative is ambiguous. The Wedding-Guest remains captive, still within the grasp of the old man's overwhelming rhetorical powers. That captivity prevents the Wedding-Guest from participating in the marriage sacrament, compelling him instead to participate in the Mariner's imaginative journey. "A sadder and a wise man, / He rose the morrow morn." ❀

Critical Views on
"The Rime of the Ancient Mariner"

MAUD BODKIN ON THE EMOTIONAL EFFECTS OF THE POEM

[Maud Bodkin is the author of *The Quest for Salvation in an Ancient and Modern Play* (1941). In the excerpt below from her chapter entitled "A Study of 'the Ancient Mariner' and of the Rebirth of Archetype," Bodkin discusses the emotional effects this poem produces in the reader.]

The Rime of the Ancient Mariner is a poem that, within its lifetime of a century and odd years, has proved its power to awaken a deep response in many individuals. Also it is a romantic poem in the full sense of that term, as expounded, for example, by Professor Abercrombie—a poem whose reality depends upon the inner experience projected into its fantastic adventures, or, in the words of Coleridge himself, a poem in which the shadows of imagination become momentarily credible through 'the semblance of truth' which we transfer to them 'from our inward nature'. Such a poem seems specially likely to reward the kind of examination proposed in these essays. To inquire concerning the emotional patterns activated in response to the poem is to inquire into the poem's meaning—in the sense of that emotional meaning which gives it reality and importance to the reader, as distinct from any truth it might convey concerning happenings in the outer world. To communicate emotional rather than intellectual meaning is characteristic of all poetry, but we may well select, at the outset of our study, poems the ground of whose appeal is most evidently the expression of the inner life. ⟨...⟩

I would propose first the question: What is the significance, within the experience communicated by *The Ancient Mariner,* of the becalming and the renewed motion of the ship, or of the falling and rising of the wind? I would ask the reader who is familiar with the whole poem to take opportunity to feel the effect, in relation to the whole, of the group of verses, from Part the Second:

Down dropt the breeze, the sails dropt down,
'Twas sad as sad could be;
And we did speak only to break

The silence of the sea!

. . . .

Day after day, day after day,
We stuck, nor breath nor motion:
As idle as a painted ship
Upon a painted ocean.

and from Part the Sixth:

But soon there breathed a wind on me,
Nor sound nor motion made:
Its path was not upon the sea,
In ripple or in shade.

It raised my hair, it fanned my cheek
Like a meadow-gale of spring—
It mingled strangely with my fears,
Yet it felt like a welcoming. ⟨. . .⟩

Mr. Hugh I'Anson Fausset in his study of Coleridge has pronounced the poem of *The Ancient Mariner* 'an involuntary but inevitable projection into imagery of his own inner discord'. Of the images of the stagnant calm and of the subsequent effortless movement of the ship, Fausset says they were 'symbols of his own spiritual experience, of his sense of the lethargy that smothered his creative powers and his belief that only by some miracle of ecstasy which transcended all personal volition, he could elude a temperamental impotence'. If we pass from considering our own response to the poem to consider with Fausset the more speculative question, what were the emotional associations in the mind of Coleridge with the imagery he used, there seems to be a good deal that confirms Fausset's interpretation.

Coleridge has told us how poignantly he felt an obscure symbolism in natural objects. 'In looking at objects of Nature,' he writes, 'I seem rather to be seeking, as it were *asking* for, a symbolical language for something within me that already and for ever exists, than observing anything new.' This is a typical expression of that attitude which Abercrombie describes as characteristic of the romantic poet—the projection of the inner experience outward upon actuality. There seems little doubt that, possessing this tendency to find in natural objects an expression of the inner life, Coleridge felt in wind and in stagnant calm symbols of the contrasted states he knew so poignantly, of ecstasy and of dull inertia.

He has told us of the times when he felt 'forsaken by all the *forms* and *colourings* of existence, as if the *organs* of life had been dried up; as if only simple Being remained, blind and stagnant'; and again, of his longing for the swelling gust, and 'slant night-shower driving loud and fast' which, 'whilst they awed'—

> Might now perhaps their wonted impulse give,
> Might startle this dull pain, and make it move and live!

So, also, the image of a ship driving before the wind is used by him as a conscious metaphor to express happy surrender to the creative impulse. 'Now he sails right onward' he says of Wordsworth engaged upon *The Prelude*, 'it is all open ocean and a steady breeze, and he drives before it'. In *The Ancient Mariner* the magic breeze, and the miraculous motion of the ship, or its becalming, are not, of course, like the metaphor, symbolic in conscious intention. They are symbolic only in the sense that, by the poet as by some at least of his readers, the images are valued because they give—even though this function remain unrecognized—expression to feelings that were seeking a language to relieve their inner urgency.

In the case of this symbolism of wind and calm we have a basis of evidence so wide that we hardly need go for proof to introspective reports of reader or poet—interesting as it is to see the confirmatory relation between evidence from the different sources. We find graven in the substance of language testimony to the kinship, or even identity, of the felt experience of the rising of the wind and the quickening of the human spirit.

—Maud Bodkin, *Archetypal Patterns in Poetry: Psychological Studies of Imagination* (London: Oxford University Press, 1934): pp. 26–27, 34–35.

PETER KITSON ON THE INFLUENCE OF THE FRENCH REVOLUTION

[Peter Kitson is a well-known scholar and the author of numerous books and articles on the Romantics. He is a contributing editor of such titles as *Coleridge and the*

Armoury of the Human Mind: Essays on His Prose Writings
and *Romanticism and Colonialism: Writing and Empire:
1780–1830.* In the excerpt below from his article,
"Coleridge, the French Revolution, and 'The Ancient
Mariner': Collective Guilt and Individual Salvation," Kitson
discusses the relevance of the French Revolution and the
origins of Coleridge's ideas on guilt and restoration.]

S. T. Coleridge's 'The Rime of the Ancient Mariner' was written
against the background of the collapse of the poet's hopes for the
improvement of mankind by political action, the ultimate failure of
the French Revolution to distinguish itself from its oppressive
Bourbon predecessors. The contribution of Coleridge's political
beliefs to this poem has never been fully appreciated. Certainly 'The
Ancient Mariner' has none of the political allusions which stud the
contemporaneous 'France: an Ode' or 'Fears in Solitude' and this has
led most critics to concur with E. M. W. Tillyard that the poem
exhibits 'a total lack of politics'. Yet given the circumstances which
gave rise to 'The Ancient Mariner', this very absence of political
content is itself political. As Carl Woodring puts it, if Coleridge's
supernatural poems are poems of escape, 'politics form a large part
of what they escaped from'.

The importance of the French Revolution to 'The Ancient
Mariner' can be seen in Coleridge's obsession with that other poet
and disillusioned supporter of revolution, John Milton. During
1795–96 he fills the Gutch memorandum notebook with allusions
and references to Toland's edition of Milton's prose works of 1698.
Coleridge had Milton's career very much in mind when writing 'The
Ancient Mariner'. Like himself, the poet of *Paradise Lost* had
witnessed the complete wreck of his own hopes for a regenerated
nation. In March 1819 Coleridge delivered a lecture on Milton and
Paradise Lost which tells us a great deal about his own state of mind.
Milton was: '. . . as every truly great poet has ever been, a good man;
but finding it impossible to realize his own aspirations, either in
religion or politics, or society, he gave up his heart to the living spirit
and light within him, and avenged himself on the world by
enriching it with this record of his own transcendent ideal'. ⟨. . .⟩

The ideas of guilt and restoration which are implicit in 'The
Ancient Mariner' were developed by Coleridge over several years and
grew out of his observation of the career of the French Revolution.

Coleridge appears to have become a supporter of the Revolution and an upholder of dissenting views of society and religion through his contact with William Frend during his time at Jesus College, Cambridge. Whatever the source of his opinions, it is clear that Coleridge became a keen supporter of the Revolution who remained loyal even during the difficult years of Robespierre's Terror. Like other British radicals Coleridge ascribed the excesses of the Revolution to the intervention of the counter-revolutionary forces who combined to destroy it in 1792. ⟨. . .⟩

There have been almost as many readings of 'The Ancient Mariner' as there are critics. Few, however, have made any real attempt to place the poem within the context of Coleridge's loss of faith in political action, a context which is demanded by Coleridge's other writings. Most critics have taken as a starting point Coleridge's contemporaneous candidature for the Unitarian ministry at Shrewsbury and have located the poem in a Christian environment. As Robert Penn Warren puts it, the shooting of the albatross 'symbolises the Fall, and the Fall has qualities important here: it is a condition of will, as Coleridge says "out of time", it is the result of no single motive'. Non-Christian evaluations of the poem have tended to follow J. L. Lowes's dictum that 'The punishment, measured by the standards of a world of balanced penalties, palpably does not fit the crime'. The moral of the poem, outside the poem, is meaningless. Such critics as E. E. Bostetter have denied that the poem contains any balanced theology; instead it shows that 'the universe is the projection not of reasoned beliefs but of irrational fears and guilt feelings'. These critics ignore the religious elements of the poem, concentrating instead on its psychological aspects. At least two critics, however, have made an attempt to locate the poem in Coleridge's political development. William Empson argues that it was the maritime expansion of colonial powers and their subsequent guilt at their treatment of other civilizations which is the poem's main theme, and J. R. Ebbatson believes that the punishment meted out to the mariner and his shipmates represents 'European racial guilt, and the need to make restitution'.

Christian readings tend to stress the redemptive aspects of the poem whereas non-Christian evaluations concentrate on the strong sense of guilt it communicates. It is not within the scope of this discussion to adjudicate between the two positions. Instead I should like to place the poem in the context of Coleridge's retreat from politics and his new-found sense of inward and individual restoration. Within this framework the elements of redemption and guilt are of paramount importance.

Coleridge was disillusioned with the French Revolution but also convinced of the depth of his own country's guilt. He had come to believe that this national and collective guilt was only a reflection of man's original sin. During the composition of 'The Ancient Mariner' Coleridge was brooding upon his own sense of personal guilt. In this sense D. W. Harding is right; Coleridge knew very well the mental depression and sense of worthlessness with which he invests his mariner in Part IV of the poem:

> Alone, alone, all, all alone,
> Alone on a wide wide sea!
> And never a saint took pity on
> My soul in agony.

The Mariner becomes aware of his own inner depravity and isolation: 'A wicked whisper came, and made | My heart as dry as dust.' It was a crime for the mariner to shoot the albatross just as it was a crime for Eve to eat the apple. It was also a crime for Coleridge to believe and encourage people to expect that mankind could improve itself by its own action unaided by grace. As R. L. Brett puts it, 'the killing of the albatross is representative of a class of which it is itself typical. It is symbolical . . . of all sin'.

—Peter Kitson, "Coleridge, the French Revolution, and 'The Ancient Mariner': Collective Guilt and Individual Salvation," *Yearbook of English Studies* 19 (1989): pp. 197, 198, 204–05.

JOHN T. NETLAND ON THE ROLES OF THE WEDDING-GUEST AND THE EDITOR

[In the excerpt below from his article "Reading and Resistance: The Hermeneutic Subtext of *The Rime of the Ancient Mariner*," John T. Netland argues that within the poem are two respondents to the mariner's strange tale, the Wedding-Guest and the gloss-writing editor, each of whom serves a particular interpretive function.]

In our attention to the Mariner's gripping narrative, we often forget that the poem is, at least on one level, about understanding—and responding to—an extraordinary tale. The poem contains a record of two such respondents: the Wedding-Guest who is compelled to listen to the Mariner, who overcomes his early resistance to the "grey-beard loon," and who emerges from the encounter deeply moved; and the gloss-writing editor who, in the written record of his reading, demonstrates a sympathetic, scholarly interest as he seeks to explain and interpret the tale, but who never shares the Wedding-Guest's affective response. This hermeneutic subtext is also apparent in the cryptic nature of the narrative itself. The tale unfolds as a mythological narrative about the supernatural, revealing a primal pattern of fall, confession, and restoration. The Mariner commits a grievous offense which, however cryptic it remains, consists of something more heinous than killing the bird: he has transgressed a moral order, the nature of which he is at first unaware and of which he remains only dimly cognizant at the end of the tale. The narrative remains a story with an elusive meaning, and translating story into ideational coherence becomes the necessary hermeneutic task, a task undertaken by the historically belated writer of the marginal glosses. Although we might expect this reader, with his apparent sympathy and scholarly acumen, to represent the ideal Coleridgean reader, we discover on the contrary that his notes do precious little to help us understand the Mariner's experience. Rather, it is the Wedding-Guest who emerges from this encounter "sadder and wiser," who, by being initiated into a profoundly meaningful (if mysterious and disturbing) human experience, demonstrates a much clearer understanding of the Mariner's experience than does the gloss-writer.

What accounts for the difference between these two respondents? Certainly one possibility, now a staple of criticism, is the distinction between knowing and experiencing: the gloss-writer is so intent upon knowing what transpired that he fails to experience the pathos of the tale in the way that the Wedding-Guest does. Yet beyond such privileging of emotional experience over cognition, the gloss-writer's failure is also an imaginative failure. There are no relevant categories in the gloss-writer's rationalistic, enlightened mind in which to place the Mariner's distinctly non-rational experience. This textual encounter between the editor and the Mariner thus problematizes the hermeneutic encounter of a modern, rationalistic reader with a distinctly premodern, myth-like text, and the hermeneutical impasse in the marginalia stems from the failure of this reader to negotiate his own ideological commitments and boundaries with those quite different values of the Mariner. In contrast to Suleiman's dissenting reader, who stops disbelieving the narrative conventions after having suspended disbelief, and to McGann, who consciously resists what he believes to be an act of ideological coercion, this gloss-writing reader simply ignores that which lies beyond his imagination.

Though virtually ignored for nearly a century after publication, the marginal glosses have generated no little interest in the twentieth century. ⟨. . .⟩ Though the voices of the Mariner and this editor were recognized as distinct, most early analyses managed to harmonize the differences. More recently, critics have seen these differences as irreconcilable and competitive. Not surprisingly, as Max Schulz notes, "deconstructionists, phenomenologists, and critical skeptics of varying hues [have seized] on the interplay between poetic narrator and prose glossist as an ironic model of the rhetorical experience that is the reader's." Yet one need not rely solely on contemporary theory to insist that the gloss notes represent an ironic point of view, for Coleridge's practice of and reflections on reading during the years in which he revised the marginalia suggest that the gloss notes can hardly be taken at face value. ⟨. . .⟩

It is not simply a tension between competing moral visions that these voices reveal. Sarah Dyck, Frances Ferguson, and K. M. Wheeler have all pointed out differences between the gloss-writer's and Mariner's moral visions: the gloss-writer's systematic attempts to attribute causality and to impose moral closure on the narrative by insisting on the primacy of the Mariner's lesson in universal benevolence; the Mariner's unsystematic, inarticulate, and likely uncomprehended experience in a world whose morality—though real—resists easy classification. Such readings properly increase our distrust of the facile ease with which the gloss notes reduce the Mariner's experience to a simple ethical lesson. Yet there is a deeper tension in this poem, a tension which becomes clearer when this dialogic relationship of text and commentary is situated in the hermeneutical and doctrinal polemics of the emerging discipline of biblical scholarship, with which Coleridge was both familiar and actively engaged. By situating the poem in the Higher Critical hermeneutical tradition, McGann alerts us to the ideological tensions between reader and text. What his analysis does not acknowledge, however, is that the poem is less syncretistic and harmonious than he suggests; rather, it contains a tension between contrasting religious imaginations—between the mystical, symbolic, irrational power of the religious sublime on the one hand and a categorical, enlightened, and rational systemization of religious experience on the other. And this narrative tension works precisely to undermine the type of modernist presumption with which McGann calls for a resistance to Coleridge's presumably outdated Christian ideology.

—John T. Netland, "Reading and Resistance: The Hermeneutic Subtext of *The Rime of the Ancient Mariner*," *Christianity and Literature* 43, no. 1 (Autumn 1993): pp. 39–40, 41.

SARAH WEBSTER GOODWIN ON THE WEDDING CEREMONY

[Sarah Webster Goodwin has written many articles on the Romantic period. She is also a contributing editor of such titles as *Death and Representation* and *The Scope of Words: In Honor of Albert S. Cook*. In the excerpt below from her article on "The Rime of the Ancient Mariner," Goodwin focuses on the often marginalized wedding ceremony as the true center of the mariner's story.]

Domesticity is not exactly what comes to mind when you read either *Frankenstein* or "The Rime of the Ancient Mariner." These are not works about *Gemütlichkeit*, plenitude, the pleasures of the hearth. If we are to look for domesticity in them, we have to turn to the margins. "The Rime of the Ancient Mariner" literally marginalizes the home, embodied in the wedding that frames the poem and whose domesticized bowers and maidens are apparently antithetical to everything in the mariner's tale. *Frankenstein* might be said to invert that structure since it opens and closes on an ocean voyage with a narrator who explicitly refers to Coleridge's poem as a guiding influence; and all three of the novel's most climactic moments occur when the monster enters a home and destroys it— one of them on Frankenstein's wedding night. Thus the structural inversion is really a mirror image: in both works domesticity is marginal, threatened, seemingly inadequate to the powers informing the central acts and mysteries that are narrated. ⟨...⟩

These works repress domesticity, and the monstrous arises from that repression. Departing from Freud's theory of the uncanny, *das Unheimliche*, in which Freud shows that the uncanny embraces both meaning of *heimlich*—the secret and the familiar—I want to reconsider the secret affinity between the domestic and the monstrous. In these works, feminine domesticity is closely aligned with kitsch, that uncanny monster that is both marginal to art and its mirror image.

Kitsch eludes easy definition; it is a term that not only censures a would-be art object, but also locates the work within a certain kind of relation to art. That relation has several dimensions in the evolution of kitsch as a critical category. First, the work of art is construed as authentic, in contrast to the inauthenticity of kitsch. Second, the inauthenticity of kitsch derives directly from its place in a postindustrial economy; this economy represents art as commodity. Thus its development in history directly parallels that of middle-class consumerism—and, not coincidentally, of Romanticism as cultural phenomenon: kitsch and Romanticism emerged at the same historical moment. ⟨...⟩ I am arguing here that kitsch is also related to gender differences, that certain kinds of kitsch are marginalized because of their links with feminine domesticity. To put it most bluntly, "high" art historically needs to leave home. As art's uncanny double, kitsch must be repressed, silenced, kept out of sight in the work that aspires to seriousness. But the very process of repression can leave its uncanny traces in the text. *Frankenstein* and "The Rime of the Ancient Mariner" are works haunted by a repressed feminine domesticity whose identity is closely related to "inauthentic" art—to kitsch. ⟨...⟩

Looked at through this lens, it would seem that the wedding at the margin of the ancient mariner's story is in fact its center—its secret care, even its obsession. That suspicion is confirmed by the grotesque female form that appears at one of the poem's turning points, the figure that approaches on the spectre ship and casts dice for the mariner's soul:

> *Her* lips were red, *her* looks were free,
> Her locks were yellow as gold:
> Her skin was as white as leprosy,
> The Night-mare LIFE-IN-DEATH was she,
> Who thicks man's blood with cold.

This is the harlot who inverts, and subverts, the wedding—who blights with plagues the marriage hearse. She has been read as the deformed mother, the object of desire distorted by the poet's guilt and rage. Any biblical or apocalyptic reading of the poem must take her into account as the Whore of Babylon, seductive but fatal, the dark counterpart to a vision of the New Jerusalem. Her complement is not only the bride, but the good mother, Mary, whose protective powers the mariner repeatedly invokes. Multiply demonic, LIFE-IN-DEATH has the bad taste to win the dice game against her presumably male opponent—and to cry out in triumph. There seems little question that hers is the triumph of the castrating female, that secret, fearful presence at the heart of the home. The mariner must encounter that presence even in the exclusively, oppressively male domain of the ship at sea. Although critics have consistently located the poem's climax in Part VII, the moment when the mariner blesses the (phallic, possibly narcissistic) water snakes, surely the encounter with LIFE-IN-DEATH is at least as central. Her dice game marks a turning point in his existence from which there is clearly no return; and, as Edward Bostetter has pointed out, the fact that it is a game of *chance* she wins is crucial to any reading of the poem's larger meaning. Perhaps because critical debate about the poem has been much exercised to define the nature and consequences of the mariner's blessing, it has paid relatively little attention to what we might call the poem's other center, its feminine one.

> —Sarah Webster Goodwin, "Domesticity and Uncanny Kitsch in 'The Rime of the Ancient Mariner' and *Frankenstein*," *Tulsa Studies in Women's Literature* 10, no. 1 (Spring 1991): pp. 93–95.

MORSE PECKHAM ON THE POEM AS A VOYAGE OF DISCOVERY

[Morse Peckham has written extensively on the Romantic period and is the author of numerous books, including *Romanticism and Ideology* and *The Romantic Virtuoso.* In the excerpt below, Peckham traces the predominant trope of a voyage of discovery to the travel literature of the 16th and 17th centuries. He argues that "The Rime of the Ancyent Marinere" is really a new type of poem exploring the relationship of the individual to his culture.]

Coleridge's claim in "France: An Ode," his response to the aggression of France towards Switzerland, that liberty could not be achieved by social instrumentalities meant that like Wordsworth he was engaged in rejecting his cultural tradition and in becoming increasingly alienated from the dominating traditions of European culture. And that is the theme of his greatest achievement, *The Rime of the Ancyent Marinere.*

The foundational trope or metaphor of the poem came from the great sixteenth and seventeenth century voyage and travel compilations of Richard Hakluyt of 1589 (enlarged 1598–1600) and those of his assistant and successor, Samuel Purchas, in 1625: a voyage of discovery the culmination of which was the voyage around the world from England around Cape Horn to the Pacific and thence back to England. To tell the story of the poem would be otiose, for everyone educated in England or the United States knows it. But the poem's interpretation is another matter. For in fact it was a new kind of poetry. In an allegorical narrative the most important proper names, and sometimes all of them, belong to an explanatory system of which the poem itself is an exemplification. In this poem there is nothing of the sort, at least in the poem's original form. Indeed, we are justified in seeking to explain the poem, to consider it as a kind of allegory in which the proper names do not belong to any explanatory system, only because the lines "And she is far liker Death than he; / Her flesh makes the still air cold" are changed in the final version (1817) to "The Night-mare LIFE-IN-DEATH was she / Who thicks man's blood with cold." The clearly allegorical proper names, capitalized by Coleridge, provides a strong instruction that the whole poem is properly considered an exemplification of some kind of explanatory system—although at first glance indeterminable—whether religious, political, metaphysical, or psychological.

With this hint it is possible to discern a pattern to the whole, and that pattern is best understood as concerned with the relation of the individual to his culture. The first step is to realize that the Mariner commits the same kind of action twice—first when he shoots the albatross which had played with the sailors and shared their food; and second when he interrupts the wedding and holds the wedding guest back from a celebration of social solidarity. Both actions are violations of community and as such are typical Romantic cultural vandalisms. This redundancy is extended when the priest to whom the Mariner confesses goes mad. Confession does not, as it should, restore the Mariner to solidarity with a community. And by a further extension of this redundancy the Mariner is condemned to eternal wandering and telling his story without receiving absolution or membership in any community.

Coleridge does not provide explanations for any of these actions and events. He is interested only in the nature of the act and its consequences. This is why the ship set out from England with no stated purpose either of exploration or of economic enterprise. Coleridge thus abstracts society, or community, from the matrix of interactions, without considering the possible purpose or goal of social relationships and patterns of interaction. So the Mariner's act is incomprehensible; Coleridge appears to be looking at Wordsworth's incomprehensible abandonments from the point of view of the abandoner, the violator. And it might even be said that the Mariner's crime (as Coleridge calls it in his 1817 gloss) is a manifestation of an alienation symbolized most traditionally by the antarctic cold, which is subsequently identified with Life-in-Death. But this cold is followed by the entrance into a new world, one into which no human had ever penetrated. The Mariner finds himself in an absolutely novel cultural condition, one in which his primary feeling is guilt as indicated by the heat, by the albatross hung around his neck instead of the cross, the emblem of Christian community, and by the death of his shipmates. He is now completely alone in a terrifyingly hideous and repulsive world. But again incomprehensibly he blesses the horrifying monsters of the world, and blesses them unconsciously. "Unaware" is Coleridge's word. Here is a parallel to the subsequent creation of Liberty by the culturally unaided individual in "France: An Ode." The albatross drops into the sea; the Mariner is freed from a culturally assigned and determined guilt. Beneath the notion of liberty in "France" lies the profound notion of the ascription of value; the Mariner's hideous world suddenly changes into a world of great beauty. Moreover it is done unconsciously. Coleridge's way of indicating with the utmost commitment that the creation of value is not a social act but one which arises from an individual's resources—resources which he does not know he has and which he cannot consciously control.

—Morse Peckham, *The Birth of Romanticism: Cultural Crisis 1790–1815*, Greenwood, Fla.: The Penkevill Publishing Company, 1986): pp. 126–28.

H. R. ROOKMAAKER JR. ON HUMANITY'S RELATIONSHIP WITH NATURE

[H. R. Rookmaaker Jr. is a well-known scholar and the author of several books, including *Synthetist Art Theories: Genesis and Nature of the Ideas on the Art of Gauguin and His Circle* (1959). In the excerpt below from the chapter entitled "Alienation Reconsidered: 'The Ancient Mariner,'" Rookmaaker argues against a moral interpretation of the poem and instead focuses on the difficulties inherent in humanity's relationship with nature.]

Many critics have tended to interpret the poem in moral terms along lines broadly indicated by Adair's statement that 'The Ancient Mariner is concerned with the existence of evil, the spiritual aridity which follows it, and the eternal wandering of the soul which is only partially redeemed'. In contrast, I will argue that the primary significance of the poem is not of a moral character, but epistemological in that it deals with an exploration of the implications of Coleridge's attitude to the relation between man and nature, as it has been outlined in the previous chapters of this study.

Before presenting my own case, I will indicate briefly some of the more influential approaches to the poem. R. P. Warren's famous essay, 'A Poem of Pure Imagination: an Experiment in Reading' may serve as an example of the more optimistic moral interpretations of the poem. He argues that the poem essentially tells 'a story of crime and punishment and repentance and reconciliation' and he characterizes its primary theme as 'the theme of sacramental vision, or the theme of the "One Life"'. In his conception the shooting of the albatross 're-enacts the Fall' in that it is 'symbolically, a murder, and a particularly heinous murder, for it involves the violation of hospitality and of gratitude . . . and of sanctity'. For this murder the mariner is subsequently punished, after which a process of reconciliation is set in motion culminating in the mariner's recognition of the 'one Life'. ⟨. . .⟩

If one believes with Warren that the poem describes an ordered, just, and ultimately benevolent universe, one can hardly avoid the vexing problem of the significance of its natural and supernatural imagery. Warren tries to impose a consistent pattern of symbolism on the imagery, but, as has been shown repeatedly by others, his attempt does not really succeed. Warren's excellent failure in this respect has made other critics wary of proposing a comprehensive interpretation of the poem's imagery. But the stakes are high: if the imagery is inconsistent or arbitrary, it must be concluded that the mariner's universe, described in terms of this imagery, is to some extent arbitrary and without order. No wonder that critics have continued the attempt to find a satisfactory symbolic pattern in the imagery. ⟨. . .⟩

It will be argued that Coleridge's preoccupation with man's relation to nature, with the difficulties inherent in his notion of nature's life-giving activity and man's passive receptivity, is also the poet's main concern in 'The Ancient Mariner'.

It may be best to recall briefly the stage of development Coleridge's thought had reached when he wrote 'The Ancient Mariner'. At this time he did not question the benevolent, divine character of the external world. He believed that if man is open to nature's influence, he will come to recognize God in nature resulting in virtue, happiness, and a true understanding of the world and its beauty. Of decisive importance is the conditional clause, 'if man is open to nature's influence': nature is the language God speaks to man, but it is up to man whether he is willing to listen to it or not.

Man can also shut himself off from nature's influence, consciously like the protagonist of Wordsworth's 'Lines Left Upon a Seat in a Yew-Tree', or unconsciously, through grief or guilt, like Margaret in 'The Ruined Cottage', or Osorio. As Coleridge had already affirmed in 1796, man is capable of 'Untenanting creation of its God', so that instead of 'a vision shadowy of Truth', he sees 'vice, and anguish, and the wormy grave, / Shapes of a dream'. If man is blind to the presence of divine light in nature, he is left with his own self-imposed darkness which he in turn projects on nature so that he becomes 'A sordid solitary thing . . . / Feeling himself, his own low self the whole', surrounded by a nature that is no more than an extension of his own mind, his own dejection or fear.

In 'The Ancient Mariner' Coleridge tried to face the implications of this reverse side of his faith in nature, tried to describe the causes and consequences of man's alienation from nature and God. If this is accepted, it will appear that the poem has its proper place in the development of Coleridge's thought and does not contradict his statements in the apparently more optimistic poems he wrote at the same time.

—H. R. Rookmaaker Jr., *Towards a Romantic Conception of Nature: Coleridge's Poetry Up to 1803: A Study in the History of Ideas* (Philadelphia: John Benjamins Publishing Company, 1984): pp. 65, 66–67, 68–69.

Thematic Analysis of
"Frost at Midnight"

Written and published in 1798, "Frost at Midnight" has traditionally been categorized as part of a group referred to as Coleridge's "conversation" poems. The basic features of these poems are a seemingly serene setting, a muted atmosphere, a distinct narrative voice that maintains a conversational manner with at least one interlocutor, and a confidential and intimate tone, as if the narrator is speaking with a close friend. Critics have often viewed these poems as requiring a knowledge of certain biographical facts about Coleridge. In his essay on the conversations poems, G. M. Harper has described the poems as "Poems of Friendship," stating that "[t]hey cannot be even vaguely understood unless the reader knows what persons Coleridge has in mind" (*The English Romantic Poets*).

Although the predominant voice in the conversation poems is the speaker's, the speaker is not self-centered. Instead, he conveys his inner thoughts and feelings, and this introspection in turn provides a point of departure for understanding the world outside the self. In a word, the speaker is meditating and, at the same time, addressing another listener. In these poems the listener is always mute for one reason or another and therefore cannot respond, as in "Frost at Midnight," where Coleridge is speaking to his infant child, Hartley.

Despite the intimacy and familiarity of the poems, they also possess an element of mystery, as will be seen in "Frost at Midnight." The speaker's communion with a mute, inanimate, or at times absent interlocutor produces this subtle supernatural dimension. Although these poems are in the guise of a conversation, they are in fact a product of a poetic imagination that sought to eliminate the barriers between the individual mind and its experience of the phenomenal world.

The source of these poems' strangeness, therefore, may spring in part from the fact that the poet combines the realistic description of a particular location with the artistic language of his innermost thoughts and feelings. This fusion of inner being with exterior world, this blending of thoughts and feelings with objects and natural phenomena, would later become Coleridge's theory of the symbol.

The structure of the conversation poems follows a basic time pattern of present-past-future, with a concluding return to the present. They begin with an initial crisis in which the poet experiences alienation from a particular, familiar location, even while he continues to exist within it.

The **first stanza** begins with a description of the speaker sitting alone at night with his sleeping baby and the quiet coziness of their interior space. "My cradled infant slumbers peacefully. / 'Tis calm indeed! So calm, that it disturbs." The natural world depicted in stanza one does not participate in the sweet repose of the child. Outside, "The owlet's cry / Came loud" and the silence of the village distresses the speaker's mind, for it is a silence that "vexes meditation with its strange / and extreme silentness." The speaker experiences a profound loneliness and separation, despite the familial surroundings in which all others sleep undisturbed. His feelings of isolation are so extreme he is unable to sustain the emotional balance necessary to enter a meditative state; instead, he is deeply distracted.

Despite these feelings, the speaker attempts to reestablish his equilibrium by focusing on the "the low-burnt fire" that "quivers not." In its all but extinguished state, the fire appears to be in sympathy with the speaker's feelings of isolation. The fire has not fully died, however, and neither has the speaker lost all hope of communication with his surroundings.

He establishes an imaginative relationship with the dying embers, sensing that they somehow share his uneasiness with the disquieting silence. "Only that film, which fluttered on the grate, / Still flutters there, the sole unquiet thing. / Methinks, its motion in this hush of nature / Gives it dim sympathies with me who live." This dwindling vestige of life, "whose puny flaps and freaks the idling Spirit / By its own moods interprets," becomes the source of possible regeneration for the speaker's dying spirits. Therefore, the poet keeps it alive in his mind as another being seeking to find itself.

Amid the dying embers of spiritual well-being and the poetic struggle to reestablish those feelings, the most important and mysterious element is Nature itself. Nature performs a religious function from the very outset of stanza one: "The Frost performs its secret ministry, / Unhelped by any wind," but we cannot see what inspires and animates the Frost to perform this office. Thus, the poet identifies the frost with his imagination, which supplies its own hope and consolation for him.

In the **second stanza**, the poet reflects on his childhood and the way in which he experienced the fluttering embers. "How, oft, at school, with most believing mind, / Presageful, have I gazed upon the bars to watch that fluttering *stranger!*" This stanza, where he describes the burning embers as a "stranger," something from which he remembers feeling alienated, contrasts sharply with his description of the very same phenomenon in the first stanza, where he is able to feel a kinship with a fire that has "dim sympathies with me who live." In the present, the fire is a friend, though symbolically it was a stranger in his childhood. However, despite the various references to childhood memories of the "stern preceptor," referring specifically to the Rev. James Boyer at Christ's College, the predominant and implicit theme of this stanza is the expectation that a close companion will soon arrive: "For still I hoped to see the stranger's face, / Townsman, or aunt, or sister more beloved."

In the next few lines the poet establishes another opposition. In contrast to the silence of the first stanza, the young boy recollected by the poet is one who was "stirred and haunted" by the ringing of the church bells, "falling on mine ear / Most like articulate sounds of things to come!" The present is silent, but the past is full of sound.

In the **third stanza**, the silence returns—"the gentle breathings, heard in this deep calm"—with the father rejoicing in the beauty of his child. "My babe so beautiful! it thrills my heart." Having achieved a communion with Nature, delighting in the stillness of the cottage, the adult poet now turns his thoughts to the infant son. He projects his imagination into a blissful future where the sweet child will live in harmonious relationship to Nature, "wander[ing] like a breeze / By lakes and sandy shores, beneath the crags / Of ancient mountain."

However, this wish for his child is in sharp contrast to his own remembrance of the feelings he experienced while growing up in the city. The imagery of that experience is expressed in terms of imprisonment. "For I was reared / In the great city, pent 'mid cloisters dim, / And saw nought lovely but the sky and stars." He wishes that his son would be fully alive to all the sensual pleasures and freedom to be found in Nature: "So shalt thou see and hear /

The lovely shapes and sounds intelligible / Of that external language which thy God / utters." In a word, Nature will respond to his son as a dear companion, delivering a message from God.

Having gone from past to future, in the **last stanza** of the poem the adult poet returns from his imaginative journey to the present time with a renewed sense of joy and rejuvenated spirits, vowing that he will never again feel alienated from Nature. "Therefore all seasons shall be sweet to thee, / Whether the summer clothe the general earth / . . . or the redbreast sit and sing / Betwixt the tufts of snow." The poem ends with the "secret ministry of frost" having performed its spiritual mission. ❀

Critical Views on
"Frost at Midnight"

JAMES K. CHANDLER ON WORDSWORTH'S
UNDERSTANDING OF COLERIDGE

[James K. Chandler is the author of *Questions of Evidence: Proof, Practice and Persuasion Across the Disciplines* (1994). In the excerpt below, Chandler cites "Frost at Midnight" to explain Wordsworth's construction of Coleridge in *The Prelude* as a man traumatized by the big metropolis and the failure of the French Revolution.]

Though Wordsworth has tactfully emphasized that he and Coleridge "by different roads, at length have gained / The self-same bourne," and though he insists that he writes to Coleridge in order to have a sympathetic ear for his own self-exploration, it is nonetheless true that Coleridge is addressed here as a man in trouble by a poet who thinks he can help. The "Coleridge" of *The Prelude* turns out to be one of those many Englishmen who have been traumatized by the "vast city" and by the failure of those revolutionary expectations which the "encreasing accumulation of men in cities" helped to create.

That this intention governs the poem from the start is suggested by Wordsworth's bracketing of the entire 1799 manuscript of *The Prelude* within allusions to "Frost at Midnight." The first allusion occurs in the original poem's second sentence:

> For this didst thou,
> O Derwent, travelling over the green plains
> Near my "sweet birth-place" didst thou beauteous Stream
> Make ceaseless music through the night and day . . . ?

The second allusion introduces the concluding address to Coleridge from which I have just quoted:

> Thou, my Friend, wast reared
> In the great city 'mid far other scenes. . . .

To understand how these allusions function in *The Prelude,* we must recall their original context. "Frost at Midnight," the prototype for "Tintern Abbey," is a dramatization of the poet's reverie as he sits before his cottage fire, his babe in his arms, on a February night. The reverie is controlled by the lore which Coleridge knows about the "film" or "stranger" fluttering on the grate: it is supposed, as his note informs us, "to portend the arrival of some absent friend." Because the film is "unquiet" on the grate, the speaker sees it as an image of himself,

> a companionable form,
> Whose puny flaps and freaks the idling Spirit
> By its own moods interprets, every where
> Echo or mirror seeking of itself,
> And makes a toy of Thought.

To the complex spatial mirroring of this situation is then added a kind of temporal mirroring, as the speaker, still under the spell of the superstition of the "stranger," now calls to mind moments from his days at school in London when, "with most believing mind," he would similarly gaze "upon the bars / To watch the fluttering *stranger.*" In such moments, moreover he would be carried back to still earlier times:

> . . . and as oft
> With unclosed lids, already had I dreamt
> Of my sweet birth-place, and the old church-tower,
> Whose bells, the poor man's only music, rang
> From morn to evening, all the hot Fair-day,
> So sweetly, that they stirred and haunted me
> With a wild pleasure, falling on mine ear
> Most like articulate sounds of things to come!

The reason why Wordsworth's allusion to this passage cannot be taken innocently is that Coleridge does not represent this reverie-within-a-reverie as a pleasant experience. It is rather an exercise in frustration, a case of unrelieved anxiety:

> So gazed I, till the soothing things, I dreamt,
> Lulled me to sleep, and sleep prolonged my dreams!
> Awed by the stern preceptor's face, mine eye
> Fixed with mock study on my swimming book:
> Save if the door half opened, and I snatched
> A hasty glance, and still my heart leaped up,
> For still I hoped to see the *stranger's* face,
> Townsman, or aunt, or sister more beloved,
> My play-mate when we both were clothed alike!

The movement of Coleridge's mind in this poem is meant to betray the profound self-*in*sufficiency that is acknowledged in the closing address to the infant Hartley, i.e., in the passage to which Wordsworth alludes at the conclusion of the 1799 MS of *The Prelude* (book 2 of the 1805 and 1850 versions):

> My babe so beautiful! it thrills my heart
> With tender gladness, thus to look at thee
> And think that thou shalt learn far other lore,
> And in far other scenes! For I was reared
> In the great city, pent 'mid cloisters dim,
> And saw nought lovely but the sky and stars.
> But *thou*, my babe! shalt wander like a breeze
> By lakes and sandy shores, beneath the crags
> Of ancient mountain, and beneath the clouds,
> Which image in their bulk both lakes and shores
> And mountain crags: so shalt thou see and hear
> The lovely shapes and sounds intelligible
> Of that eternal language, which thy God
> Utters, who from eternity doth teach
> Himself in all, and all things in himself.

Wordsworth alludes to Coleridge's poignant confession of city-caused anxiety and emotional instability in order to offer himself to Coleridge as a man who already has wandered like a breeze by lakes and sandy shores, beneath mountains and clouds. He also offers himself as a poet who has learned "far other lore" than that which informs the mind of Coleridge, and he will go on in *The Prelude* to show how the power of this natural lore saved him from psychic harm in a time of trouble. If *The Prelude* can become "A power like one of Nature's," as Wordsworth hoped, it could then be a source of natural lore for debilitated urbanites who suffer what Coleridge suffers.

"Frost at Midnight" was written in February 1798, in the midst of the two-month period during which Wordsworth conceived his great program for poetry. *The Prelude* was begun later in that year. During the latter part of the winter of 1803–4, when Coleridge's health suffered its sharpest decline, Wordsworth worked hard on the poem to expand it to its planned five-book form. During his stay with the Wordsworths in December and January, Coleridge was, in W. J. Bate's words, "very ill, probably from an overdose of narcotics" and "suffering with repressed guilt" over his decision to leave the country. At some point between 6 March and 29 March, just before

Coleridge did leave the country, Wordsworth decided to expand the poem to include his own debilitating experiences in London and in France. Not long after this decision was taken, probably in late March, Wordsworth composed for *The Prelude* a second farewell to his friend and auditor, the longest address of its kind in the entire poem. The opening blessing recalls the conclusion of book 2:

> Speed thee well! divide
> Thy pleasure with us; thy returning strength
> Receive it daily as a joy of ours;
> Share with us thy fresh spirits, whether gift
> Of gales Etesian, or of loving thoughts.

> —James K. Chandler, *Wordsworth's Second Nature: A Study of the Poetry and Politics* (Chicago: The University of Chicago Press, 1984): pp. 240–43.

MARY JACOBUS ON THE CONTINUITY OF THE IMAGINATION

[Mary Jacobus is a well-known scholar and the author of numerous books and articles on the Romantics. Her books include *Romanticism, Writing and Sexual Difference: Essays on the Prelude* and *First Things: The Maternal Imaginary in Literature, Art and Psychoanalysis*. In the excerpt below from the chapter "'Tintern Abbey' and the Renewal of Tradition," Jacobus discusses "Frost at Midnight" as a poem about the interior life of the imagination, analogous to Wordsworth's "spot of time" or remembrance of childhood, which records the continuity of the imagination despite the changes brought about by growth and time.]

For all that 'Tintern Abbey' owes to the past, its most important debt is to the poetry written by Wordsworth and Coleridge themselves during the first half of 1798. 'The Pedlar' provided the impulse towards a statement of belief, 'Frost at Midnight' provided an impressive model for the kind of poetry which Bowles had failed to write, and which Wordsworth himself had never previously attempted—the poetry of inner life. In 'Frost at Midnight' the familiar themes of loss and renewal are subsumed into a new concern with the power of the mind to link past, present, and future in organic relationship. Like Bowles's *Monody*, Coleridge's poem is an elegy for a past self; but another principle of organization is now at work—not the meditative-descriptive parallel, but imagination. Where earlier Conversation Poems had centred on moments of transcendental experience or insight, 'Frost at Midnight' centres on a Wordsworthian 'spot of time', a vivid recollection of childhood experience which looks forward to Part I of the 1799 *Prelude*. Both poems invite entry into the poet's consciousness, and both use the processes of self-realization—their recognition of becoming as well as of changing—to demonstrate the essential continuity of inner life. ⟨. . .⟩

In Coleridge's poem, the 'secret ministry of frost' becomes an analogue both for the silent, inner workings of thought, and for the transforming power of the imagination. As the natural world is transfigured, the world of the individual changes its face from one of solitude and self-imprisonment to one of relationship and freedom.

Coleridge's opening, like the start of 'Tintern Abbey', suggests a mind turned inward; the external world is merged into the calm of thought:

> THE Frost performs its secret ministry,
> Unhelp'd by any wind. The owlet's cry
> Came loud—and hark, again! loud as before.
> The inmates of my cottage, all at rest,
> Have left me to that solitude, which suits
> Abstruser musings: save that at my side
> My cradled infant slumbers peacefully.
> 'Tis calm indeed! so calm, that it disturbs
> And vexes meditation with its strange
> And extreme silentness. Sea, hill, and wood,
> This populous village! Sea, and hill, and wood,
> With all the numberless goings on of life
> Inaudible as dreams!

'Sea, hill and wood . . . Sea, and hill, and wood'—the repetition is lulling, but not sleepy. Coleridge's surroundings are 'Inaudible as dreams', but his younger self achieves the vividness of a present reality; 'the numberless goings on of life' have been displaced by memory. ⟨. . .⟩ The silence that 'disturbs / And vexes meditation' in 'Frost at Midnight' suggests both the heightened awareness of midnight solitude, and the way in which silence has itself become the most important sign of mental life. In Hazlitt's phrase, it is a 'busy solitude'. In 'Frost at Midnight', the suppressed paradox—a disquieting quiet—signals the suspension of ordinary sense-perception. ⟨...⟩

The major achievement of the Conversation Poem is its fusion of subjective experience and philosophic statement. Feeling and meaning interpenetrate, and the discursiveness of *The Task* gives way to a kind of poetry that is both more economical and more profound. In 'Frost at Midnight', the random reflections of Cowper's fire-gazing become the basis for a poem about the power of the imagination to bring mind and nature into creative relationship. The point of reference for its movement to and fro in time is the 'stranger', the sooty film on the grate—described by Cowper with the mock-seriousness which allows him to comprehend the ordinary within his Miltonic idiom:

> Nor less amused have I quiescent watch'd
> The sooty films that play upon the bars
> Pendulous, and foreboding in the view
> Of superstition prophesying still
> Though still deceived, some strangers near approach.

To Coleridge, the restless play of the film becomes a metaphor for the mind's unceasing activity. But the projection of his own life onto other things has troubling implications. Is adult consciousness self-reflecting, self-imprisoned, no longer a means of effecting entry into either the world of the imagination or the world beyond the self?

> Only that film, which flutter'd on the grate,
> Still flutters there, the sole unquiet thing,
> Methinks, it's motion in this hush of nature
> Gives it dim sympathies with me, who live,
> Making it a companionable form,
> With which I can hold commune. Idle thought!
> But still the living spirit in our frame,
> That loves not to behold a lifeless thing,
> Transfuses into all it's own delights,
> It's own volition, sometimes with deep faith,
> And sometimes with fantastic playfulness.
> Ah me! amus'd by no such curious toys
> Of the self-watching subtilizing mind,
> How often in my early school-boy days,
> With most believing superstitious wish

Presageful have I gaz'd upon the bars,
To watch the *stranger* there! and oft belike,
With unclos'd lids, already had I dreamt
Of my sweet birthplace, and the old church-tower,
Whose bells, the poor man's only music, rang
From morn to evening, all the hot fair-day,
So sweetly . . .

The recollection of 'the hot fair-day' releases Coleridge's imagination
into the free flow of memory. The vivid 'spot of time' experienced by
the child is in contrast to the adult's mental processes ('the self-
watching subtilizing mind'), and his daydream paradoxically brings
a fuller encounter with reality. The adult's mind experiences itself:
the child's imagination relives the whole stretch of the fair-day
('From morn to evening . . .').

> —Mary Jacobus, *Tradition and Experiment in Wordsworth's* Lyrical
> Ballads *(1798)* (London: Clarendon Press, 1976): pp. 118–20, 121–22.

PAUL MAGNUSON ON THE POEM'S POLITICAL CONTEXT

[Paul Magnuson is a well-known scholar and has written
extensively on the Romantic period. His works include
Wordsworth and Coleridge: A Lyrical Dialogue (1988) and
Reading Public Romanticism (1998). In the excerpt below
from his article, "The Politics of 'Frost at Midnight,'"
Magnuson discusses the poem within a political context, a
reading which depends on its location within the same
volume as the other conversation poems and on the public
debate in which it participates.]

I will elaborate an argument that "Frost at Midnight" is a political
poem if it is read in the dialogic and public context of Coleridge's
other poems and the political debates of the 1790's. A comparison of
"Frost at Midnight" with other Coleridge poems yields a conclusion
contrary to House's. But before I ask about the significance of a
Romantic lyric, I want to ask about its location: Where is it? and
Who conspired to put it there? The method that I will follow argues
that a lyric's location determines its significance, and to change a

poem's location is to change its dialogic significance, sometimes radically. "Frost at Midnight" was written in late February 1798. It is commonly read as an intensely subjective, meditative lyric written in isolated retirement and reflecting the isolated consciousness of its author; or it is read in the context of Coleridge's other Conversation Poems such as "The Eolian Harp" and "This Lime-Tree Bower," and it echoes the themes of those poems with which it was grouped as "Meditative Poems in Blank Verse" in *Sibylline Leaves* (1817); or it is read in the context of Wordsworth's lyrics, particularly "Tintern Abbey." But it was first published in the fall of 1798 as the final poem in a quarto volume that began with two explicitly political poems: "Fears in Solitude" and "France: An Ode." These two poems were also written early in 1798, and "France: An Ode" was published in the *Morning Post*, April 16. The quarto was published by Joseph Johnson, the radical bookseller, in the early fall after Coleridge met him in late August or early September while he was on his way to Germany with Wordsworth.

I propose to locate "Frost at Midnight" in the context of the other poems in the volume and to locate the volume in the context of the political debates conducted in the popular press. ⟨. . .⟩ I will be comparing Coleridge's poems with other written material that is not often considered in a traditional explication; I draw upon the political pamphlets and political journalism, which implies that a Romantic lyric participates in the ordinary language of the day. For this contexual reading there is no distinction between an aesthetic language that is unique and separate from ordinary language. ⟨. . .⟩

To put all this in a simpler way: I will be looking at the public Coleridge and the public location of the poem. Our reconstructions of Coleridge in this century are based upon the publication of his notebooks and letters, by our knowledge of the scholarship that has traced his reading, and by our knowledge of his later career. None of these were available to his contemporaries, whose comments make the history of the reception of the poem and whose debates constitute the context of its publication. ⟨. . .⟩

For a reading of "Frost at Midnight" in the public dialogue, the crucial dates are those of the composition of the volume in late August or early September 1798, when Coleridge first met Joseph Johnson. The dates of the writing of the poem are relatively insignificant, because the purposes of publication are more important than Coleridge's original intentions in drafting the individual poems. To publish, in the 1790's, was inevitably to enter a public debate. In August, when the volume was composed, both author and publisher were under attack from the press and the government. Joseph Johnson, whose name appeared boldly on the title page, had been placed on trial in the Court of the King's Bench and convicted on July 17 for selling Gilbert Wakefield's *A Reply to Some Parts of the Bishop of Llandaff's Address to the People of Great Britain*. His indictment reads in part: "Joseph Johnson late of London bookseller being a malicious seditious and ill-disposed person and being greatly disaffected to our said Lord the King . . . wickedly and seditiously did publish and cause to be published a certain scandalous malicious and seditious libel. . . ." Although he had been found guilty, sentencing was postponed for many months for obvious reasons. At the hearing on his sentence, he would have to produce evidence of his good behavior in any plea for leniency. His sworn statement at the hearing claimed "that where he could take the liberty of doing it, he has uniformly recommended the Circulation of such publications as had a tendency to promote good morals instead of such as were calculated to mislead and inflame the Common people." ⟨. . .⟩

The public debate that the volume entered was composed of a rhetoric of purposeful duplicity, distortion, and personal attack, and Coleridge was constantly in the sights of the *Anti-Jacobin*, which contains many attacks on him although often Coleridge is not mentioned by name. One of its major aims was to expose the errors in the liberal press, which it ranged under three categories: lies, misrepresentations and mistakes. Its Prospectus promised to present "Lies of the Week: the downright, direct, unblushing falsehoods, which have no colour or foundation whatever, and which at the very moment of their being written, have been known to the writer to be wholly destitute of truth." Yet its own rhetoric was that of parody and distortion. The early numbers contained essays on Jacobin poetry, whose major targets were Southey and Coleridge. ⟨. . .⟩

"Fears in Solitude" calls upon his countrymen to rise and defeat the impious French. "France: An Ode" deplores French aggression while retaining admiration for the Revolution. And "Frost at

Midnight" concludes with six lines that were later deleted. The "silent icicles" will shine to the moon

> Like those, my babe! which, ere to-morrow's warmth
> Have capp'd their sharp keen points with pendulous drops,
> Will catch thine eye, and with their novelty
> Suspend thy little soul: then make thee shout,
> And stretch and flutter from thy mother's arms
> As thou would'st fly for very eagerness.

The public and dialogic significance of "Frost at Midnight" in the fall of 1798 was that it presented a patriotic poet, whose patriotism rested on the love of his country and his domestic affections. Coleridge specifically instructed Johnson to send a copy of the volume to his brother, the Reverend George Coleridge. As the reviewer in the *Monthly Review* (May 1799) put it, "Frost at Midnight" displays "a pleasing picture of virtue and content in a cottage," hardly a penetrating critical comment of interest to us in these days of deconstruction and hermeneutics, until one recognizes that the word "content" implies the negation of its opposite. Coleridge is not discontent, not ill-disposed to the existing state of society; he is not, therefore, seditious.

> —Paul Magnuson, "The Politics of 'Frost at Midnight,'"
> *The Wordsworth Circle* 22, no. 1 (Winter 1991): pp. 3–4, 6.

JERROLD E. HOGLE ON THE POEM'S GOTHIC ELEMENTS

[Jerrold E. Hogle is the author of *Evaluating Shelley* (1996) and *Shelley's Process: Radical Transference and the Development of His Major Works* (1988). In the excerpt below from his article "The Gothic Ghost as Counterfeit and Its Haunting of Romanticism: The Case of 'Frost at Midnight,'" Hogle discusses the way in which a "high romanticist" such as Coleridge actually depends in "Frost at Midnight" on the "low" elements of Gothic writing, such as spectral figures and fantastic trappings.]

Thanks especially to Anne Williams, we are no longer in any doubt that the Gothic and what we call the "Romantic" in poetry are symbiotically interrelated, especially in some of the best-known English poems of the 1780's through the 1820's. Many features of verses by Wordsworth, Coleridge, Scott, Byron, Keats, and Percy Bysshe Shelley, as well as aspects of works by Anna Letitia Barbauld, Mary Robinson, and Joanna Baillie, turn out (we now see) to be Gothic quite frequently and hauntingly, even in the sense that they replay quasi-archaic images and spectres used, not just in older "graveyard poetry," but throughout the short tradition of neo-Gothic fiction and drama that was nominally launched in Horace Walpole's *The Castle of Otranto,* which was given the pointed and quite marketable subtitle *A Gothic Story* (making it the first book to use the label) in 1765. At the same time, though, thanks equally to the work of Michael Gamer, we are also aware that so-called "High Romantic" writing, particularly by Wordsworth and Coleridge, ironically situates itself as relatively "high cultural" poetry by distinguishing itself explicitly from the "lowness" and threatening excess of Gothic novels and plays (even as Coleridge in particular wrote quasi-Gothic drama in *Remorse*). The Gothic, particularly the horror Gothic in its pre-"shilling shocker" mode in the 1790's, is clearly one target—called "frantic novels"—among "the gross and violent stimulants" against which Wordsworth sets off his and Coleridge's non-incendiary and "natural" poems suited in their contemplative moderation to "the discriminating powers of the mind," according to the Preface to the Second Edition of *Lyrical Ballads.* ⟨...⟩

I want to suggest here why it was that both of these inclinations arose at the same time and what it means that at least some "Romantic" writing was extensively based on the very Gothic spectres whose "manufacture" and "cheap" mobility some of the "high Romantics" strove forcefully to condemn. After all, there is a reason why Gothic images and ghosts would seem "manufactured" to such writers beyond the fact that Gothic fictions were being widely printed and sold in the "lower culture" marketplace. From the very start of the "Gothic" mode as soon as it began reusing that much older label as a marketing device, there has been a very fake and mechanically reproduced quality to much of what the Gothic offers, whether it be in novels, plays, paintings, or Gothic-revival architecture. ⟨...⟩

A vivid case in point, since I can focus on only one example in this short space, is Coleridge's much-discussed "Frost at Midnight," particularly in its initial 1798 printing, though much of what I find there also applies to the better-known final version of this poem. The key image through which Coleridge's autobiographical speaker connects his current awareness to his memories is, of course, "that film, which flutter'd on the grate" and "Still flutters there" as an "unquiet thing" in the fireplace of a "cottage" surrounded by "Sea, hill, and wood." Coleridge provides a footnote to this image, even in 1798, intimating that "in all parts of the kingdom these films are called *strangers*, and supposed to portend the arrival of some absent friend," and this allusion to circulating folklore soon justifies the poem's recollection of "school-boy days" when the speaker "watched the *stranger* there" by gazing on the film in a different fireplace of another time. As Humphry House noted decades ago, to be sure, all these moments recall Book IV ("The Winter Evening") in William Cowper's *The Task* (1785), where "have I quiescent watched / The sooty films that play upon the bars . . . in the view / Of superstition prophesying still . . . some stranger's near approach." But Coleridge gothicizes the image far more than Cowper did, partly by turning the film *into* the ghostly "stranger," partly by making it hauntingly "companionable" as an "unquiet thing" vaguely echoing the past, and partly by allowing that fluttering shade, on the basis of its use in folklore and poetry already circulating for many years, to float from being a film on a cottage grate in 1798 to seeming a "*stranger*" in an earlier schoolroom fireplace, to taking the form of a "*stranger's* face" appearing to enter the schoolroom from his distant "birthplace" at a moment when the "school-boy" speaker may have been halfway between dreaming and waking. This figure partakes of virtually all the qualities we have noted in a Gothic ghost of the counterfeit. It harkens back into the past towards a seemingly natural reference-point with a definite social status, yet it circulates far beyond that old foundation as a floating signifier able to attach itself to different beings and objects again and again, all with the aid of texts that have recontextualized the figure more than once (paralleling the history of the word "Gothic," as we have seen). At every point, the "*stranger*" refers to what is already a mere signifier at the earlier stage, even when the term seems attached to a face from the speaker's earliest youth and thus not really a stranger. The face the poem finally arrives at is a sequence of shifts under the overall label of "*stranger*," a movement across a "Townsman, or aunt, or sister" from his "birthplace" that does not decide among them, even as the word *"stranger"* becomes a spectre of a counterfeit (as well as "uncanny") by being the sign of someone who has come to seem unfamiliar (or re-coined) but is not ultimately strange to the speaker in the oldest location he remembers.

Hence Jan Plug can write of "the rhetoric" in "Frost at Midnight" that, even as "it attempts to literalize itself" (in a face, for example), "the literal figure . . . never arrives," just as it never truly does in the Walpolean Gothic. The poem's later hope that the "Dear babe" in the present cottage may have a less displaced life than the speaker has had—a hope given some encouragement by the poem's seeming capacity to trace the *"stranger"* back to a primordial person and "birthplace"—all of this is already and continually haunted by how the mechanically reproduced *"stranger"* remains other than itself and always a ghost of what is spectral to begin with, already textualized, and at least partly unauthentic at every turn. The rising terror hinted early in the poem when the "unquiet" film reminds the speaker of just how "dim" the original foundations of memory have become may indeed be turned into a sense of continuity bridging the separate stages of the growing self.

> —Jerrold E. Hogle, "The Gothic Ghost as Counterfeit and Its Haunting of Romanticism: The Case of 'Frost at Midnight,'" *European Romantic Review* 9, no. 2 (Spring 1998): pp. 283, 284, 287–88.

JONATHAN BATE ON POLITICAL THEMES WITHIN THE POEM

[Jonathan Bate is a well-known scholar who has written extensively on the Romantic period. His books include *Romantic Ecology: Wordsworth and the Environmental Tradition* (1991) and *The Romantics on Shakespeare* (1992). In the excerpt below from his article, "Living with the Weather," Bate focuses on the way in which the "political" themes of domestic virtue and the need to defend Britain from the anticipated invasion of 1798 are interwoven within "Frost at Midnight," elucidating the differences between being and dwelling.]

With its thatch-eves, mossed cottage-trees and morning mistiness, Keats's imaginary dwelling-place is built upon the Nether Stowey cottage-home described by Coleridge in "Frost at Midnight." The verbal echoes sound from the closing section of "Frost":

> Therefore all seasons shall be sweet to thee,
> Whether the summer clothe the general earth
> With greenness, or the redbreast sit and sing
> Betwixt the tufts of snow on the bare branch
> Or mossy apple-tree, while the nigh thatch
> Smokes in the sun-thaw; whether the eave-drops fall
> Heard only in the trances of the blast,
> Or if the secret ministry of frost
> Shall hang them up in silent icicles,
> Quietly shining to the quiet Moon.

At the micro-political level of ideology, "Frost at Midnight"'s celebration of snug (though surely not smug) domestic virtue may be related to a Burkean defense of "home" against French revolutionary innovation during the invasion-fear of 1798; at the macro-political level of ecosophy it is a meditation on the relationship between being and dwelling, achieved through a subtle interplay of what Serres calls *les deux temps*.

The secret ministry of the frost (weather) is the exterior analogue for the equally secret interior ministry of the memory (time). As the frost writes upon the window-pane, so memory writes the poet's identity. By the end of the night both the environment of the cottage and the ecology of the poet's mind will have subtly evolved. The poet has learnt to dwell more securely with himself, his home and his environment. But the structure of the evolution is that of a topological network, not a Newtonian sequence of action and reaction. The distinction I have in mind here is one made by Serres in his *Éclaircissements*. If you take a handkerchief and lay it flat to iron it, you can define fixed distances between points on it: this is the geometry of the classical age. But if you crumple up the same handkerchief to put it in your pocket, two points that were far apart can be near together or even superimposed on one another: this is the topology of networks. For Serres, both time and the weather are structured according to this kind of topology.

Chaos theory has a name for these relationships: they are fractal. I believe that as Keats had an intuitive knowledge of the importance of illusory excess as a principle of community ecology, so Coleridge had an intuitive knowledge of the fractal structure of time and weather. How may we measure the motions of "Frost at Midnight"? The pattern of the frost; the flickering of the flame and the flapping of the film on the grate; the flowings of breeze, wave, cloud, thaw-steam, eve-drop and icicle? They are fractal. The poet's abstruser musings have dim sympathy with these motions because they have a similar structure, in that the poem's temporal structure is not classically sequential, but crumpled like Serres' handkerchief in such a way that it makes manifest neighborings ("voisinages" [*Éclaircissements*]) which are invisible to the modern Constitution.

The temporal structure may be simplified as present-past-future-present. In its imagining of the baby Hartley's future, the poem proposes an ideal mode of dwelling in which the human subject is set into a new relationship with the objects of nature:

> But *thou*, my babe! shalt wander like a breeze
> By lakes and sandy shores, beneath the crags
> Of ancient mountain, and beneath the clouds,
> Which image in their bulk both lakes and shores
> And mountain crags.

The child is imagined as becoming like the weather, the breeze which plays across both land and water. But, more than this, the Enlightenment form of spatial perception is shattered: the parallelism of "beneath the crags" and "beneath the clouds" breaks down the rigid distinction between solid and vaporous matter, while the image of the mountains and clouds imaging the lakes reverses the classical structure of substance and shadow (real mountain above, illusory image reflected in water below). The dislocation—the *pliage*—is such that it no longer seems appropriate to talk about human subject and natural object. The Cartesian subject/object distinction is made to vanish.

The imagined relationship between Hartley and nature is like the articulated relationship between Samuel and Hartley. The italicized *thou* strives to replace the dialectic of subject and object with an intercourse of I and thou. Where the subject/object relationship is one of power, the I/thou is one of love. Bond and tie replace mastery and possession. An ecofeminist language of nurture and care, as against male technological exploitation, is again apposite. What is truly radical about "Frost at Midnight" is Coleridge's self-representation as a father in the traditional maternal posture of watching over a sleeping baby. In ecofeminist terms, this realignment of gender roles clears the way for a caring as opposed to an exploitative relationship with the earth.

—Jonathan Bate, "Living with the Weather," *Studies in Romanticism* 35, no. 3 (Fall 1996): pp. 445–47.

Thematic Analysis of
"Christabel"

Published in 1816, "Christabel" is a poem written in two parts, Part I written in 1798 and Part II in 1800. The poem was influenced by Percy's *Reliques of Ancient Poetry,* a collection of medieval ballads—short, highly dramatic poems that originated in the folk tradition. These ballads were at one time transmitted orally among illiterate people, and they included pieces of Gothic horror such as vampirism, violence, eroticism, and strange, gloomy settings. The Gothic influence is plain in the work of novelist Matthew Lewis, whose book *The Monk* Coleridge discussed in an article for *The Critical Review* of February 1797. In his introduction to *The Monk,* John Berryman states that "this grotesque school helped usher in the English Romantic Movement and debauched taste without ever really participating in the glories of the movement unless in the book before us."

These tales also contain elements of medieval literature, such as haunted castles, magic spells, and treacherous journeys. "Medievalism" was much concerned with stories of unrequited love as an essential part of the Middle Ages' courtly love tradition. The poem's central character, Christabel, who searches for her long-absent lover, is very much in the same tradition.

Part I begins with the tale of "the lovely lady" Christabel, the daughter of the rich but ineffectual Baron, Sir Leoline. (This name is ironic, for it implies all the attributes that the character lacks, namely the strength and courage of a lion.) In the poem's opening scene, Christabel is in a dark and foreboding forest that is transformed into a unnatural landscape when the distinction between night and day is ominously disturbed. Though it is "the middle of night by the castle clock, . . . the owls have awakened the crowing cock." An important part of this brooding setting is Sir Leoline's dog, "a toothless mastiff bitch," who howls at the clock. Some say the dog is haunted by "my lady's shroud," the symbol of Christabel's deceased mother.

From the outset of the poem, we encounter a rhetorical device that is repeated several times. A narrative voice poses a question to the reader and then responds to its own question. In the first occurrence, the narrator questions the "true" circumstances of the world of "Christabel": "Is the night chilly and dark? / The night is chilly, but not dark." In so doing, the narrative voice effectively heightens the suspense and drama about to unfold.

Within the forest is a huge oak covered with "moss and the rarest mistletoe," a reference to a pre-medieval, Celtic system of belief that venerated this parasitic plant when it grew on an oak tree. The landscape of the poem is definitely feminine in nature, with a "huge, broad-breasted, old oak tree" and a "mastiff bitch"—and the nature of that femininity is dangerous and duplicitous, as will soon become apparent when Christabel encounters Lady Geraldine.

Indeed, the oak tree appears to take on the personality of Geraldine when it seems to be moaning. However, we soon learn that Geraldine herself is the one who cries out for help. In an important inversion of the medieval tradition, a woman is the one who comes to her rescue, none other than Christabel who is likewise in great distress. "There she sees a damsel bright / Dressed in a silken robe of white, / . . . A lady, so rich clad as she— / Beautiful exceedingly." Christabel reassures the lady: "Then Christabel stretched forth her hand, / And comforted fair Geraldine." Christabel is the substitution here for such valiant, legendary knights as Sir Lancelot and Gawain; she demonstrates feminine chivalry and courteous behavior toward Geraldine. "'O well, bright dame! May you command / The service of Sir Leoline; / and gladly our stout chivalry / Will he send forth and friends withal.'" The reference to "our stout chivalry," especially indicates Christabel's full participation in the chivalric code of honor.

However, her promise of Leoline's protection is ironic, since in fact he is old and frail, in no position to offer anyone protection. Nor, for that matter, is the castle a place of safe haven. Christabel's acknowledges as much when she tells Geraldine what to expect when they enter the castle: "'Sir Leoline is weak in health, / And may not well awakened be, / But we will move as if in stealth, / and I beseech your courtesy, / This night, to share your couch with me.'"

Our first subtle hint of Geraldine's treachery is at the very point of her entrance into the castle. Christable, in an inverted marriage-rite, lifts Geraldine, "a weary weight, / Over the threshold of the gate"; a legend is associated with the old marriage custom, namely that a witch cannot cross the threshold on her own because it has been blessed against evil spirits. Once in the castle, their way to the bedroom is equally fraught with hints of danger; in "a fit of flame," Christabel only sees "the lady's eye, and nothing else." The damsel in distress, Geraldine, has begun a process of transformation into an evil spirit. When they finally arrive at Christabel's chamber, "carved with figures strange and sweet," Christabel offers Geraldine "a wine of virtuous powers," which her deceased mother made from wildflowers. But Geraldine rejects the offer and instead banishes the mother's spirit from the room, presaging her evil intent to take possession of the innocent and unsuspecting Christabel. "'Off, woman off! This hour is mine— / though thou her guardian spirit be, / . . . 'tis given to me.'"

Geraldine does eventually drink the "virtuous" wine, but she still intends to take possession of Christabel. That possession, while primarily of spirit, may possibly be sexual as well, although the poet only hints at this. Once Christabel has undressed, Geraldine does the same and reveals her truly hideous nature. "'In the touch of this bosom there worketh a spell, / Which is lord of the utterance, Christabel!'" The hideous aspect of Geraldine's body is her "mark of shame," which, she tells Christabel, will soon be fully disclosed. Geraldine indicates that she and Christabel are united in a connection where she exercises the most powerful of all control—a complete dominion over Christabel's speech. Thus, her control over Christabel is not only magical, but rhetorical as well, a terrible and cruel fate of mythic dimensions such as that suffered by Echo, a figure from Greek mythology who was metamorphosed into stone and whose only speech was to echo someone else's words.

Now under Geraldine's awful spell, Christabel has become her captive, "the lovely lady's prison," and Part I concludes with Christabel's wish for divine intervention against this evil spirit. "But this she knows, in joys and woes, / That saints will aid if men will call." That remains to be seen.

Part 2 begins with a reminder of the spiritually and physically ineffectual Baron who lives in a world devoid of faith and any hope of salvation. "'Each matin bell,' the Baron saith, / 'Knells us back to a world of death.'" True to his fallen nature, the world within the castle is devoid of hope, filled with religious symbols that are mere trappings, emptied of all spiritual significance. There is "the drowsy sacristan" who counts slowly, merely to fill up the time, and "[t]hree sinful sextons' ghosts which hover about," "[w]ho all give back, one after t'other, / The death note to their living brother," suggesting that Sir Leoline carries the burden of their transgressions.

Christabel, who has awoken from her sleep at the conclusion of Part I, now feels refreshed because she "hath drunken deep / Of all the blessedness of sleep!" She is confused by Geraldine's presence, and she erroneously believes herself to have committed a mortal sin. Christabel proceeds to lead the sorceress to Sir Leoline. True to his fallen status, he cannot see properly (the eyes traditionally believed to be the gateway to the soul), and because of this defect, he is blind to Geraldine's evilness. "With cheerful wonder in his eyes / The lady, Geraldine, espies."

He greats her with great respect and ceremony and, when he soon discovers that Geraldine is the daughter of his long-lost friend, Sir Roland, the tyranny of history repeating itself is revealed. We are told that the rupture in the friendship between Leoline and Roland was due to a particular form of rhetorical violence—it was the direct result of lies spread by malingering tongues—although we are not told the specific content of those lies. "But whispering tongues can poison truth; / And constancy lives in realms above."

The "madness in the brain" caused by the loss of friendship resembles various accounts of King's Arthur's madness when the fellowship and trust of his roundtable was destroyed by deceit. "Each spake words of high disdain / And insult to his heart's best brother."

As Leoline remembers Roland, his inability to truly see Geraldine causes his specious regeneration at the expense of his daughter. "Sir Leoline, a moment's space, / Stood gazing on the damsel's face: And the youthful Lord of Tryermaine / Came back upon his heart again."

However, not all the inhabitants of the castle are so easily deceived. The Bard Bracy, whom Leoline has commanded to spread the news of Geraldine's rescue, has had a nightmare of his own, of "a bright green snake . . . Close by the dove's [Christabel's] head it crouched." As a result of his dream, he refuses to embark on his journey. Meanwhile, the evil Geraldine with "[a] snake's small eye blinks dull and shy . . . / And the lady's eyes they shrunk in her head, / . . .

And with somewhat of malice, and more of dread, / At Christabel she looked askance! —"; Christabel can only passively reflect back "[t]hat look of dull and treacherous hate."

But the trance ends abruptly, and Christabel begs that the Baron banish Geraldine, although Christabel, still under her curse, cannot speak of what she knows. But, alas, she cannot get Sir Leoline to see the truth. "And turning from his own sweet maid, / The agèd knight, Sir Leoline, / Led forth the lady Geraldine."

The **last section** of the poem, Coleridge's ending of Part 2, may seem wholly unconnected and irrelevant to the narrative that precedes it, but it makes sense if we understand it as a "companion" poem offering yet another version of the fundamental problem of "Christabel." The poem's references to a small child, "a limber elf, / Singing, dancing to itself" is thought to be Coleridge addressing his own infant Hartley, the "fairy thing with red round cheeks." In this short poem, however, the father's love is so excessive that it is transformed into its opposite: "And pleasures flow in so thick and fast / Upon his heart, that he at last / Must needs express his love's excess / With words of unmeant bitterness."

The lesson here—the same lesson lost on Sir Leoline—is that one must be vigilant of both words and thoughts, for though they may seem harmless enough, yet they will return with a deadly power. "Perhaps 'tis pretty to force together / Thoughts so all unlike each other . . . To dally with wrong that does no harm . . . Such giddiness of heart and brain / Comes seldom save from rage and pain, / So talks as it's most used to do." ❁

Critical Views on
"Christabel"

DENNIS M. WELCH ON THE THEME OF INCEST IN
THE POEM

[Dennis M. Welch is the author of numerous articles on the Romantic poets. His work includes "Blake's *Songs of Experience:* The World Lost and Found" and "Blake's Book of Los and Visionary Economics." In the excerpt below from his article "*Christabel, King Lear,* and the Cinderella Folktale," Welch discusses the poem as a ballad, the narrative elements of which are revisions of the paternal abuse found in Shakespeare and the fairytale, which identify the poem's most terrifying theme of incest.]

Source studies of Coleridge's mysterious ballad *Christabel* have been numerous and yet tentative. In the well-researched and well-known *Road to Tryermaine,* Arthur Nethercot admits that he "has not found any one whole story on which . . . the poem depends." Similarly, Kathleen Coburn asserts that "no central fable behind it has ever been found. . . . the traditional fables on which the narrative parts are based have been all lost sight of." In spite of such remarks, however, several source-hunters and critics have shown that the ballad includes numerous folktale elements. Indeed, Coleridge himself, recognizing in the *Biographia Literaria* the broad and checkered reception of *Christabel* "among literary men" even before its actual publication, acknowledged with some chagrin that the ballad "pretended to be nothing more than a common Faery Tale." Given this acknowledgment and the considerable evidence (explored in the following pages) that the ballad deals with the paternal abuse of Christabel (and *not* merely her repressed sexual fantasies, which other critics have emphasized), this essay argues that a major source underlying Coleridge's poem is the Cinderella folktale. For variations of this tale have dealt with similar abuse and quite probably influenced the ballad through his broad reading and knowledge and especially his interest in Shakespeare's *King Lear,* which itself includes significant aspects of the Cinderella legend. Although there are many variations of the legend, which have developed in European and other cultures, several of the variations have elements in common that Coleridge would have recognized. But, interestingly, he tried to de-emphasize some of these elements both in his criticism of *King Lear* and in his ballad. In the following pages I shall discuss variations of the folktale most akin to the play and the ballad, indicate relevant parallels between these works and their common source, and argue that the ballad's provenance helps confirm that its true though horrifying subject matter is father-daughter incest.

According to Marian Cox's seminal study of the Cinderella story, the "unlawful marriage" or relationship—a euphemism for incest between a father and daughter—characterizes one group of the story's variants and "has been utilized in the legendary history of Christian saints, in a number of medieval romances, and in . . . mysteries based on the same." For example, in the "Constance Saga," from which the medieval romance *Emare* derives, a young maiden was rejected by an unnatural father—not unlike Christabel near the end of her fragmentary tale, where Sir Leoline turned "away from his own sweet maid." And just as Leoline had once loved Christabel "so well," so in *Vita Offae Primi* an ancient king of York had loved his daughter to excess. ⟨. . .⟩

⟨A⟩s Alan Dundes observes, "Many [Cinderella] folktales begin with the queen or original mother already dead" or absent. This factor was central to one of the most important of all Cinderella tales, the legend of St. Dipne; and, as I will show, it was important to *King Lear* and especially *Christabel*. According to J. A. S. Collin de Plancy, Dipne was the lovely daughter of a pagan Irish king. After her mother died Dipne remained devoted to her memory—just as Christabel remains devoted to her deceased mother ("O mother dear! that thou wert here"). But the king—a lustful though grief-stricken man, whom Sir Leoline closely resembles in his "wroth" and "madness"—tried to induce Dipne to marry him. As he became more insistent, she sought solace at her mother's grave and counsel from her confessor, who advised her to delay the king until she could flee. ⟨. . .⟩

In a study of *King Lear* in 1934, James Bransom insinuated that an "incestuous passion" by the king for one of his daughters may have influenced his behavior. In a letter to Bransom, Freud agreed, suggesting that "the secret meaning of the tragedy" involves the king's "repressed incestuous claims on a daughter's love." But in

"Delusions and Dreams in Jensen's 'Gradiva,'" which was published (in 1907) long before he wrote to Bransom, Freud has raised suspicions about Lear although he doubted the king's culpability, referring to the love-test at the beginning of the play as "an improbable premiss." ⟨...⟩

Nonetheless, the suggestions of Freud and Bransom concerning the tragedy have been taken up by more recent scholars—and with considerable persuasiveness. For example, Arpad Pauncz has argued that "Lear not only loves his daughters; he is also in love with them, especially the youngest one." When Cordelia shrinks from him, his anger and outrage toward her, which anticipate the reactions of Sir Leoline toward his daughter in Part II of *Christabel*, implicate the king's real desire. As S. C. V. Statner and O. B. Goodman aver, "Cordelia's instinctive withdrawal ... begets Lear's guilt-ridden rage, and he just as instinctively tries to cover the shame of having touched a forbidden place." Thus, ironically at the very same time this father angrily disclaims his "paternal care," "Propinquity," and "property of blood" in Cordelia, he uses words that imply a "barbarous Scythian" appetite for "his generation." Regarding the play's opening love-test specifically, Mark Taylor says that Lear tries "to assert his control over the one daughter whom he loves, who has come of age, [and] who is separating herself from him"—just as Christabel seeks to do from Sir Leoline despite her lover's untimely absence.

—Dennis M. Welch, "*Christabel, King Lear*, and the Cinderella Folktale," *Papers on Language and Literature* 32, no. 3 (Summer 1996): pp. 291–92, 293–94, 294–95.

MARGERY DURHAM ON CHRISTABEL'S AMBIGUITY

[Margery Durham is the author of "The Mother Tongue: *Christabel* and the Language of Love." In the excerpt below from her article, Durham discusses the ambiguity of Christabel's character when she vacillates between innocence and guilt. Durham relates that ambiguity to recent psychoanalytic theory that indicates the infant's relationship to the mother is the source of symbol formation and language. Thus, this is a way to understand that ambiguity.]

At the time of its publication a reviewer declared *Christabel* "the most obscene Poem in the English language." Coleridge replied, "I saw an old book in Coleorton in which the Paradise Lost was described as an 'obscene poem,' so I am in good company." In its portrayal of innocence mixed with depravity, *Christabel* draws readers into its gothic atmosphere, and there it leaves them, intrigued and bewildered. Like most readers, I am puzzled by the way in which Coleridge clouds the innocence of his central female figure. The ambivalence he suggests can be understood, I think, by reading the poem in the light of certain passages in the poet's notebooks, where his entries around the time he composed *Christabel* define topics in which he was deeply, even passionately interested. Most relevant to the poem are his speculations about associative thought, as it might function in the origin of both speech and moral choice. In the notebooks Coleridge speculates that language may develop from the physical contact between infant and mother. For Coleridge, culture begins at the breast, and language is indeed the mother tongue.

A considerable body of psychoanalytic theory recognizes the infant's relationship with the mother as the source of symbol formation and therefore of language and culture, and since Coleridge himself is credited with coining the word "psycho-analytical," it seems all the more reasonable to inquire whether any of the current theories can yield insights into his poem. Since the time of Freud and his earliest associates, Melanie Klein and those who have developed the implications of her work have further advanced our understanding of the individual's relationship to culture, and the tensions they describe in this relationship are, I believe, analogous to the ambivalence one finds in *Christabel*. Klein's definition of the alternative ways, which she terms "manic" and "depressive," by which these tensions are resolved also helps us to interpret Coleridge's work. I will therefore compare the poem with both Coleridge's notebook speculations and Klein's more systematically developed theory. Relevant to this comparison is the poem's thematic resemblance, in its consideration of a fall from innocence, to *Paradise Lost*, and this parallel provides a mythic resolution of the dilemmas, logical and psychological, which Coleridge depicts. ⟨...⟩

Klein began her work with the common psychoanalytic assumption that all formation of symbols (all fantasy, all conceptualization, and therefore all mental relationship to the outside world) is a projection of the infant's sense of the mother's body. Ernest Jones had pointed out that nonmaternal experience can provide a pleasure similar in quality to that received from the mother. Then, when access to the original pleasure is blocked, the infant can redirect its desire to the analogous experience. Cradling and suckling thus replace the womb. These pleasures can yield to the enjoyment of solid food, and in time to babbling, to speaking, even to writing poetry. From this redirection Klein reasoned not only that the outside world is "the mother's body in an extended sense," but also "that symbolism is the foundation of all sublimation and of every talent, since it is by way of symbolic equation that things, activities and interests become the subject of libidinal phantasies." From the symbolization of infantile conflict and desire in children's play and in art, she developed her theory of reparation, according to which civilization actively remodels the world into a sublimated version of the infant's original pleasure.

Klein also found that the procedure could go wrong, and it is here that her theory first illuminates *Christabel*. If the original source of pleasure fails and no analogous equation has been made, then the former pleasures become equated with potentially analogous ones within a category of unfulfillment and therefore of pain. The child then withdraws from both the painfully tantalizing mother and the analogous outside world, and the result is paranoid delusion and inhibition, including as one extreme form the speech-inhibiting psychosis now termed autism. Putting the matter rather simply: feeding problems can thus create stuttering and, at last, silence. Most important for our study of *Christabel*, Klein maintains that neurosis and sublimation are inversions of each other and, she adds, "for some time the two follow the same path" from original pleasure to possible alternatives and back—for better or worse—to the child. ⟨...⟩

At best, however, poetry, music, politics—all the civilized arts— become the means of creating, on the cultural level, a maternal equivalent. As we reshape the world to our satisfaction, Klein maintained, we try to recreate the life-giving environment that a mother can no longer provide, and our standard of comparison (outside the womb) is our recollection of the earliest moments at the breast. Aesthetic balance may suggest such analogous pleasure, and I shall argue that *Christabel* also symbolizes the conflicts within the reparative struggle.

—Margery Durham, "The Mother Tongue: 'Christabel' and the Language of Love." In *The (M)other Tongue: Essays in Feminist Psychoanalytic Interpretation*, eds. Shirley Nelson Garner, Claire Kahane, and Madelon Sprengnether (Ithaca, N.Y.: Cornell University Press, 1985): pp. 169–70 and 172–73.

AVERY F. GASKINS ON THE POEM AS BOTH A VERSE DRAMA AND A GOTHIC PARODY

[Avery F. Gaskins has written extensively on the Romantic period. His articles include "Coleridge: Nature, the Conversation Poems and the Structure of Meditation" and "Wordsworth's Stolen Boat: Some Problems of Interpretation." In the excerpt below from his article "Dramatic Form, 'Double Voice,' and 'Carnivalization' in 'Christabel,'" Gaskins discusses the poem as a type of verse drama containing more than one narrative voice and, at the same time, a poem that can be read as a parody of the Gothic novels in which the authority of established customs and institutions are subverted.]

In the fall of 1797, Coleridge finished a verse drama *Osorio* as he was also continuing work on his share of *Lyrical Ballads*. Among a number of poems in varying stages of completion upon which Coleridge worked at this time was "Christabel." Constructing a dramatic text for *Osorio* had left him with the habit of developing action through dialogue, especially questions and answers, a habit which he carried over into the writing of Part I of "Christabel." The result is a kind of hybrid text which is not drama, but has some of the feel of drama. For example, after using just thirteen lines setting the scene, some unidentified narrator begins a series of dialogues with a second unidentified narrator in the form of questions and answers:

> Is the night chilly and dark?
> The night is chilly, but not dark.
> The thin gray cloud is spread on high,
> It covers but not hides the sky.
> The moon is behind, and at the full;
> And yet she looks both small and dull.
> The night is chill, the cloud is gray:
> 'Tis a month before the month of May,
> And spring comes slowly up this way.

Exchanges such as this dominate Part I up to The Conclusion and are used by the author in the ways he might have used a single, omniscient narrator: to add further detail to the setting, to advance the action, to establish motives for the actions of characters, and to call special attention to important moments.

It may occur to some persons that these exchanges may not be dialogues at all and that the questions posed are merely rhetorical devices utilized by a single narrator. To such a suggestion, I would have a number of answers. First, the narrator would have to establish a presence or persona as Byron does for himself in *Don Juan* before using rhetorical questions for effect. In the thirteen lines leading up to the first exchange, no such persona has been established. Second, since there is already firmly set up in the opening lines a pattern of narration which is assertive, there was little economy for the narrator to have broken in with a question to himself or the reader. Rather than letting line 15 "The night is chilly, but not dark" serve as an answer, if the narrator had moved to it directly, the story could have been narrated just as effectively. There must have been another reason for introducing the question at that point, and I feel it was to establish a questioner. Third, although a question such as "Is the night chilly and dark?" may seem rhetorical since the questioner could have had the answer merely by observing, there are many others which seem to be genuine requests for information that the questioner does not have. For example, the questioner has to be told why Christabel is outside the castle by herself and at night and in the bedroom scene requests an interpretation of Geraldine's aside and to whom it is addressed. ⟨. . .⟩

The narrators speak the language of pious gossips. Their role in the story is to be feckless observers, often horrified or morally outraged at what they are observing, but without the power to intercede. In a number of places when they sense that Christabel is being morally or physically threatened, they are reduced to ritualistic prayer, "Jesu, Maria, shield her well!" In The Conclusion to Part I, as they reflect on the moral implications of what has transpired in Christabel's bedroom, they become indignant and do a great deal of clucking about. After establishing in the opening that "It was a lovely sight to see / The lady Christabel, when she / Was praying at the old oak tree," they lament the fallen condition of Christabel:

> O sorrow and shame! Can this be she,
> The lady, who knelt at the old oak tree?
> And lo! the worker of these harms,
> That holds the maiden in her arms
> Seems to slumber still and mild,
> As a mother with her child.
> A star hath set, a star hath risen,
> O Geraldine! since arms of thine
> Have been the lovely lady's prison.

They understand their own lack of power to correct the situation and must rely on the hope that Christabel herself will turn to prayer and bring about her own salvation: "And this she knows, in joys and woes, / The saints will aid if men will call: / For the blue sky bends over all!" ⟨...⟩

That "Christabel" may have parodic qualities has not escaped the notice of critics. Both Edward Duffy and Edward Dramin have suggested that "Christabel" may be a parody which has as its target the Gothic Novel. Duffy finds the parody in the characterizations, and Dramin feels the entire work parodies the major conventions of the genre.

However, as has already been stated, "carnivalization" uses parody, but goes beyond it in the sociological and ideological implications it creates, and in "Christabel," I can find parodic overtones here and there that work toward Bakhtinian "carnivalization." The objects in these cases are Sir Leoline and the class he represents. Since the manuscript of "Christabel" is a fragment lacking a conclusion, the action leading up to where the narrative stops has the potential of developing into a genuine domestic tragedy concerning an aristocratic family, or a parodic treatment thereof, and parodic language, where it is found in the poem, creates the effect of carnivalization.

Without imputing any conscious intent on Coleridge's part, I should like to suggest that the carnivalization of the De Vaux household may be a by-product of Coleridge's radical political activities from 1795 to 1798. The Pantisocracy scheme had been an attempt to escape the class structure of England and set up a more democratic society in America. Since 1795, he had been making a number of public and private statements attacking privileged classes and urging governmental reform. During this period, Coleridge exchanged letters with the radical, John Thelwell, who had been tried for treason for supporting the French Revolution and advocating the overthrow of aristocratic power in government. His admiration for Thelwell was so great that in July of 1797, just as he was beginning to write "Christabel," he invited Thelwell to come visit him in Nether Stowey with the idea that he might settle there permanently and the two men might exchange ideas more frequently and easily.

—Avery F. Gaskins, "Dramatic Form, 'Double Voice,' and 'Carnivalization' in 'Christabel,'" *European Romantic Review* 4, no. 1 (Summer 1993): pp. 2–3, 4, 7.

ROSEMARY ASHTON ON COLERIDGE'S INDECISIVENESS IN REGARDS TO GERALDINE

[Rosemary Ashton is the author of *George Eliot: A Life* and *The Mill on the Floss: A Natural History*. In the excerpt below from her biography of Coleridge, Ashton discusses some of the reasons for Coleridge's difficulties in finishing "Christabel," difficulties which are in part attributable to what she sees as his indecisiveness concerning the guilt of Lady Geraldine. She cites biographical evidence to account for that indecisiveness.]

Coleridge just could not find, or create, the conditions under which he could finish 'Christabel'. 'I tried & tried, & nothing would come of it', he confessed in a moment of plain, unvarnished truth-telling in an otherwise complicated and contradictory account to Josiah Wedgwood on 1 November. A notebook entry for 30 October speaks eloquently of his problem: 'He knew not what to do—something, he felt, must be done—he rose, drew his writing-desk suddenly before him—sate down, took the pen—& found that he knew not what to do.'

Wordsworth, too, saw the problem clearly enough. Surely Coleridge is the subject of a fragment he wrote at this time:

> Deep read in experience perhaps he is nice,
> On himself is so fond of bestowing advice
> And of puzzling at what may befall,
> So intent upon baking his bread without leaven
> And of giving to earth the perfection of heaven,
> That he thinks and does nothing at all.

It was in Volume II of *Lyrical Ballads* that Wordsworth included 'A Character, in the antithetical Manner', which Coleridge recognized as a 'true sketch' of himself. In addition to the 'weight' and 'levity' and the 'bustle and sluggishness' Wordsworth discerns in his friend's face there is the following telling paradox:

> There's indifference, alike when he fails and succeeds,
> And attention full ten times as much as there needs. ⟨...⟩

The unfinished poem 'Christabel' presents the student of Coleridge with several problems. Questions arise about how it would have ended and about its metre, which Coleridge claimed was experimental and new. Though not published until 1816, the poem was known to, and admired by, a number of Coleridge's acquaintances from Carlyon and others who heard him declaim Part I in the Hartz Mountains in 1799 to his many readings of the two parts in literary circles in the Lakes and later in London between 1800 and 1816. Several manuscripts in different hands survive; and the two most successful poets of the age, Scott and Byron, heard it read from a manuscript and imitated it in poems of their own which *preceded* the original in their date of publication.

We have therefore a case of a poem existing in slightly variant forms which were, in a sense, public property before publication. (*The Prelude* is, of course, a greater example of the same phenomenon.) 'Christabel' is a nightmare narrative with a Gothic setting, a supernatural aspect, and an unsolved mystery. Thus far it has affinities with 'The Ancient Mariner'. But there are striking differences too. The mystery in 'Christabel' is whether the Lady

Geraldine, who casts a spell on the heroine, is herself the innocent victim of an evil enchantment or a kind of incarnation of evil. What there is of the poem raises the question, but does not answer it.

In Part I Geraldine, whom Christabel finds in a wood by moonlight, says she has been abducted by 'five warriors' and has 'lain entranced' in some versions, or 'lain in fits' in others. She is invited into Christabel's father's castle, with repeated crossing of thresholds: 'they crossed the moat', 'over the threshold of the gate', 'they crossed the court', 'they passed the hall'. Once over the final threshold and inside Christabel's chamber, the strange lady engages in a muttered verbal tussle with the spirit of Christabel's dead mother. 'Off, wandering mother! Peak and pine!' says Geraldine in an echo of one of Macbeth's witches, as she puts a malignant spell on Christabel, who thereafter is unable to warn her father about this dangerous guest.

Christabel has been initiated into guilt and needs to be saved. The question remains unanswered as to how this would have happened. Coleridge would presumably have had to decide not only whether Geraldine was evil in herself or under another's spell, but also how her influence was to be negated. At some point after 1816 he apparently told Gillman that in the continuation which he went on promising in every edition from 1816 on, except the last in 1834, Geraldine was to have been defeated by the return of Christabel's absent lover.

We can make a guess about why Coleridge found it impossible to finish the poem. At its centre is the heroine's initiation into what seems like sexual guilt. She acts hospitably and is violated by Geraldine. Famously, Christabel gets into bed and watches Geraldine undress. There follows the well-known stanza which caused Shelley to scream and which influenced Keats in the dream scenes of both 'Lamia' and 'The Eve of St Agnes':

> Beneath the lamp the lady bowed,
> And slowly rolled her eyes around;
> Then drawing in her breath aloud,
> Like one that shuddered, she unbound
> The cincture from beneath her breast:
> Her silken robe, and inner vest,
> Dropt to her feet, and full in view,
> Behold! her bosom and half her side—

[Are lean and old and foul of hue]
A sight to dream of, not to tell!
O shield her! Shield sweet Christabel!

The line in brackets appears only in certain manuscript versions, one of which Hazlitt saw and gleefully restored (slightly misquoting it) in his review of the poem in 1816. He used its omission from the published version to suggest both the strong sexual element in the poem and Coleridge's timidity in handling it: 'There is something disgusting at the bottom of his subject, which is but ill glossed over.' Of the many parodies of 'Christabel', that by William Maginn in *Blackwood's Magazine* in 1819 picks up something, boldly making Geraldine a man in disguise. The bewildered Christabel finds herself pregnant, and Maginn asks cheekily:

Pale Christabel, who could divine
That its sire was the Ladie Geraldine?

This is all good, if not clean, fun. It also gets to the heart of 'Christabel' as a poem which gives expression to sexual guilt and compulsion.

Coleridge was a prey to guilty nightmares of emotional and sexual desires. Such experiences lie behind the pseudo-sexual attraction-cum-repulsion in 'Christabel' which Hazlitt was the first to spot. The Gothic setting with its melodramatic and potentially comic elements—the owls, the crowing cock, the castle clock, the mastiff bitch, the midnight excursion, the ghost of Christabel's mother—is used by Coleridge much as the Gothic novelists used such trappings, as a distancing device to render the sexual and the sinful acceptable subjects.

—Rosemary Ashton, *The Life of Samuel Taylor Coleridge: A Critical Biography* (Cambridge, Mass.: Blackwell Publishers, 1996): pp. 182, 183–85.

JENNIFER FORD ON CHRISTABEL'S DISTURBED SLEEP

[Jennifer Ford is the author of *Coleridge on Dreaming*. In the excerpt below, Ford discusses "Christabel" in terms of a poetical description of disturbed sleep, elements of which are so disturbing that Christabel is haunted even when she is awake. Ford cites biographical evidence that explains why Coleridge's treatment of sin in this poem contradicts his moral beliefs; the poem was written during the period of the *Lyrical Ballads*, a project for which Coleridge's contribution was to write poems of the supernatural.]

Some poems did arise from that long illness, most notably 'The Pains of Sleep'. Thomas Poole commented that 'The Pains of Sleep' was a 'magnificent poetical description of disturbed sleep', But other poems included with the publication of 'The Pains of Sleep' may also have arisen from the illness. Christabel, too, becomes the subject for a poetical discussion of disturbed sleep. Her retreat to the solitude of the woods is very similar to her retreat within a world of dream and sleep. She ventures out, 'a furlong from the castle gate', to pray for the safety of her lover, but she also ventures into the somnial space of her mind, where, in versions of the poem drafted between 1797 and 1801, she moans and leaps as she dreams of her knight. Coleridge, as poet, also effects a double retreat: first into the world of imagination to write the poem, and second, into the fitful sleep of Christabel, with which he empathises. This sleep is encountered not merely in Christabel's sleeping life: she recognises features of it when she thinks she is awake. As Geraldine undresses, the narrative poet reveals how her

> silken robe, and inner vest,
> Dropt to her feet, and full in view,
> Behold! Her bosom and half her side—
> A sight to dream of, not to tell!

Perhaps the 'sight' of Geraldine is akin to Christabel's dreams of her beloved knight, dreams which make her 'moan and leap' and which cannot be freely articulated because they belong in a special somnial space. Such visions and dreams are inexorably unutterable. When the night has passed, and Christable awakens and greets her father, she does not seem entirely sure that she has awoken, for the power of her dream-world is still so strong, as is the power of Geraldine: 'Christabel in dizzy trance, / Stumbling on the unsteady ground— / Shudder'd aloud, with a hissing sound.' The dizzy trance, and the earlier references to moaning and groaning in sleep, suggest that Christabel is no stranger to disturbed sleep: in fact, with 'open eyes' she is described as 'Asleep, and dreaming fearfully'. In this dizzy trance, Christabel is said to be bereft of her thoughts—'her thoughts are gone'—in much the same way as, when she first awoke, she was in such a 'perplexity of mind' that she thought she had sinned. The remnants of her uneasy dream, and the ease with which the somnial space is apparently invoked in waking life by Geraldine, are significantly stronger in the earlier drafts of the poem. Her retreat into the forest and into fearful dreams closely parallels Coleridge's notion of a 'wild storehouse' of poems, a space which houses poetic materials.

Despite his letter to Poole, Coleridge was not always confident of his ability to gain access to those strange and often painful regions of the mind. Often, he did not want to gain access at all, for those regions were totally incompatible with his conscious morality. There are countless instances of the shocking realisation that there seem to be two different parts of the self, a division which is most potently manifested in and through the processes of dreaming and in dreams themselves. This realisation was particularly evident in times of deep despair, caused by his opium taking. In a letter to Matthew Coates, from December 1803, Coleridge complains of

the Horrors of my Sleep, and Night-screams (so loud & so frequent as to make me almost a Nuisance in my own house [)] seemed to carry beyond mere Body—counterfeiting, as it were, the Tortures of Guilt, and what we are told of the Punishments of a spiritual World—I am at length a Convalescent—but dreading such another Bout as much as I dare dread a Thing which has not immediate connection with my Conscience.

His genuine lack of knowledge as to why the 'Horrors' of his sleep visit him is counterbalanced by the implied realisation that those same horrors must be in some way connected to his conscience and to his own behaviours. Illness and the onslaught of yet more dreadful dreams are described as parallel fears. The want of a connection between what is dreamt and what is conscious to the self during waking life becomes indicative of a self which is perceived as fundamentally dislodged and disrupted: the experience of dreams, an experience which is intensified in nightmares, creates the potential for the paradoxically total fragmentation of the self. That Coleridge dreads and describes such a dream as 'a *Thing* which has no immediate connection with my Conscience' (my emphasis) immediately indicates the extent to which the dream can divide the

mind into two entirely different regions with entirely different
moralities: those 'Tortures of Guilt, and what we are told of the

> instrumental~~ly~~ity of a series of appropriate and symbolic visual and
> auditual Images spontaneously rising before him, and these so clear
> and so distinct as at length to ~~become~~ overpower his first suspicions
> of their *subjective* nature and to become *objective* for him—i.e. in *his
> own* belief of their kind and origin—still the Thoughts, the
> Reasonings, the Grounds, the Deductions, the Facts illustrative or in
> proof, and the Conclusions, remain the same!

What Coleridge extracts from his hypothesis is both the *validity* of
Swedenborg's facts and conclusions and the *incorrect reasoning*
under which those conclusions were formed. Because Swedenborg
was in a unique dreaming state, and because there were certain
faculties within his mind that were still functioning as though he
were fully awake, he was unable to distinguish what he saw from
what he thought he saw: images both clear and distinct from his
own mind are eventually seen as objective. ⟨. . .⟩

As a poet whose primary concerns in the *Lyrical Ballads* were to
be 'directed to persons and characters supernatural', Coleridge
shows an interest in witchcraft and apparitions that becomes even
more intriguing. A comment he made about *Christabel* is revealing
of his thoughts on ghosts and apparitions. In October 1804, in
a cryptic note written three years after the poem, he makes a
tantalising reference to Geraldine's character: 'Saturday Morning . . .
a most tremendous Rain storm with Lightning & Thunder, one
Clap of which burst directly over . . . Vivid flashes in mid day, the
terror without the beauty. —A ghost by day time / Geraldine.' Years
later, on 1 July 1833, he claimed that the reason why he had not yet
finished *Christabel* was not because he did not know how to finish
it, but rather because he could not 'carry on with equal success the
execution of the idea—the most difficult . . . that can be attempted
to Romantic Poetry— . . . witchery by daylight'. Although this
comment has often been seen as another attempt to rationalise
why he had not completed the poem, it is also highly likely that
Coleridge's reasoning is quite correct. For over thirty years, he
attempted to understand the often cited/sighted occurrences of
ghosts, witchcraft activities and visions. If he had not yet
ascertained in his own mind the exact explanation for such
phenomena, he could not finish his poem.

His description of Geraldine as a 'ghost by day time' sheds light on his thinking on dreams and visions, and the ways in which an understanding of witchcraft could further elucidate the mysteries of dreams. His comment also reveals the important connections he perceived between the studies of witchcraft and those on dreaming. From the time that Geraldine encounters Christabel by the 'broad breasted old oak tree', and particularly those times surrounding awakening and sleeping, it seems that it is indeed the 'true witching time'.

—Jennifer Ford, *Coleridge on Dreaming: Romanticism, Dreams and the Medical Imagination* (New York: Cambridge University Press, 1998): pp. 46–47, 96–97.

Thematic Analysis of
"Dejection: An Ode"

Written and published on October 4, 1802, upon the occasion of William Wordsworth's wedding, "Dejection: An Ode" was originally a verse letter to Sara Hutchinson. Coleridge was hopelessly in love with her, although at the same time he was unhappily married to Sara Fricker. (Coleridge once stated in a letter that Sara Fricker was the one "whom I love best of all created Beings," but in fact, they were ill-suited for one another both emotionally and creatively.)

At the time of the poem's creation, Coleridge was also beset by a series of troubles: a succession of debilitating illnesses, increased dependence upon opium, and anxieties about what he conceived to be a decline in his poetic imagination. These themes can all be found in the "Dejection Ode." The poem laments dreams and desires that have seemingly passed.

Coleridge wrote the poem immediately after hearing the beginning of Wordsworth's great poem on the same subject, "Ode: Intimations of Immortality." In the early stanzas of that poem, Wordsworth imagines himself as a child seeing the world "apparelled in celestial light," yet knows that while "[t]he sunshine is a glorious birth; / But yet I know, where'er I go, / That there hath past away a glory from the earth." Coleridge sought to articulate these same feelings. He transformed an intimate letter into a more "public" arena in which he could analyze and come to terms with his own dejection about the eclipse of his poetic imagination. Ironically, despite Coleridge's anxieties about poetic failure, in "Dejection: An Ode" he brilliantly uses his poetic powers to interweave the themes of lost imagination and disillusioned love.

The structure of the poem is yet another vital interpretive key. In its most simple terms, the genre of this poem is an ode, a poem that in the ancient Greek world was intended to be sung or chanted. The ode was a complexly organized poem that was created for important state functions and ceremonies; thus, it was a mode of public address. The format of "Dejection: An Ode" is based on Pindar's odes, poems that were written between 522 and 442 B.C. as formal celebrations of the panhellenic athletic festivals. This poetry commemorated athletic victories, which the Greeks held in high esteem as the greatest of human achievements. The odes included an announcement of victory, praise for the champion, an invocation to the gods, and praise of the athlete's city and family. Also incorporated within these celebratory poems were reminders of the victor's mortality, a prayer to ward off bad luck, an awareness of the pitfalls of vanity and the dangers of provoking envy in the gods, and the importance of inherent excellence. Pindar's odes are written in regular stanzas—a strophe, an antistrophe, and an epode. The strophe is the initial component that the Greek chorus chanted while moving from one side of the stage to another, followed by a metrically-identical antistrophe, which was chanted in accompaniment to a reverse movement and lead up finally to the epode, which the chorus sung while standing still.

Coleridge admired the "profound Logic" and organization of Pindar's odes. Ultimately, however, he transformed his verse-letter into an irregular ode according to the English tradition that substituted the tripartite stanzas into a structure of turn, counter-turn, and stand, a series of balanced opposites. This genre had attained popularity in the 17th century with Abraham Cowley's *Pindarique Odes,* in which Cowley attempted to capture the spirit and tone of Pindar rather than formally imitating the classical poet. In the 18th century, the great formal odes began with John Dryden in such works as "Ode for St. Cecilia's Day." The ode became the vehicle for expressing the sublime, lofty thoughts of intellectual and spiritual concerns. Coleridge combined the formality of the genre with irregular lines that are relaxed and colloquial, enabling the poet to move between external world and the world of his imagination.

"Dejection: An Ode" begins with the ominous lines from the "Ballad of Sir Patrick Spence," which serve to introduce a mysterious and disconcerting sense of vague yet ominous foreboding. "And I fear, I fear, my master dear! / We shall have a deadly storm." In using the ballad as a preface to the ode, Coleridge acknowledges the English appropriation of the ancient genre, as well as his own creative intervention. An ode would have originally been intended for an aristocratic audience attending a state function, while the ballad is a simple song based on "folklore" and transmitted orally among illiterate people. Unlike the ode of antiquity, the ballad does not give attention to details of setting but rather focuses on dramatic intensity, which aims to stir up the emotions of its listeners.

Coleridge's creative power took these two disparate literary forms and united them.

In the first lines of the **first stanza**, the speaker formally acknowledges the validity of the English ode when he speculates whether the bard of "Sir Patrick Spence" really could predict the weather: "Well! If the bard was weather-wise / . . . This night, so tranquil now, will not go hence / Unroused by winds." This is more than mere speculation on the speaker's part; it is a wish that perhaps he will receive the necessary yet violent gesture to stir his own imagination. As things are at the moment, he is almost lifeless, languishing beneath "the dull sobbing draft" while he prays that the wind will blow "upon the strings of this Aeolian lute" (a popular metaphor for poetic inspiration). As the velocity of the storm increases, his wish intensifies as he hopes that what is foretold will come to pass. "I see the old Moon foretelling / The coming-on of rain and squally blast/ And oh! That even now the gust were swelling, / And the slant night shower driving loud and fast / . . . Might startle this dull pain, and make it move and live!" The speaker is inspired and enchanted by the sublime aspects of Nature. The majesty of torrential rains will resurrect his dejected spirit back to life. The poet uses the external world as a barometer of his own internal state. He demonstrates an ability to move quickly and adeptly between these two "places."

In **stanza 2**, the speaker's plaintive voice discusses an almost death-in-life state of being: "A grief without a pang, void, dear, and drear / A stifled, drowsy, unimpassioned grief / Which finds no nature outlet, no relief." The arid and stilted atmosphere depicted here bears strong resemblance to the "painted ocean" of "The Rime of the Ancient Mariner." The speaker's "genial spirits" have abandoned him, so that his body and spirit have lost their vital connection.

The speaker also reveals another deep longing as he addresses what we may assume is the object of his unobtainable love, Sara Hutchinson. "O Lady!, in this wan and heartless mood, / . . . Have I been gazing on the western sky, / . . . And still I gaze—and with how blank an eye!" His unrequited love is poignantly expressed as the speaker describes how very far he is from fulfilling his desire: "Those stars, / . . . Now sparkling, now bedimmed, but always seen: / . . . I see, not feel, how beautiful they are!" So dejected is the speaker's spirits that he seems to be consigned to an eternal punishment of merely looking, yet never arriving, at his destination. Nothing less than rebirth can be the antidote for such severe depression, and he has little hope of being united with the woman whom he addresses. "O Lady! We receive but what we give, / And in our life alone does Nature live: Ours is her wedding garment, ours her shroud." The speaker's juxtaposition of wedding garments with images of burial rites points to the speed with which one set of circumstances can be radically altered to its opposite.

Stanza 5 brings a slight shift in tone, for here we find at least the memory of happier days. The speaker remembers a former time when body and soul were united. This shift in atmosphere is signaled through the magnificent and brilliant images of light, both natural and celestial: "This light, this glory, this fair luminous mist, / This beautiful and beauty-making power. / . . . Joy, Lady! Is the spirit and the power, / Which wedding Nature to us gives in dower / A new Earth and new Heaven." Nevertheless, a great space still yawns between the speaker and the fulfillment of his wishes, a distance that is expressed with great poignancy, alluding to the fading visionary light of the young man in Wordsworth's "Intimations Ode": "There was a time when, though my path was rough, / This joy within me dallied with distress." In an allusion to Shakespeare's *The Tempest*, the speaker expresses a wish for a magical transformation of a tragic turn of events into a joyous outcome: "And all misfortunes were but as the stuff / Whence Fancy made me dreams of happiness." Thus the stage is set for a complete reversal of the speaker's psychological state in the next long stanza, Stanza 6.

Stanza 7 begins with the speaker banishing the demons with which he has been bedeviled. "Hence, viper thoughts, that coil around my mind, / Reality's dark dream!" He takes determined action to lift himself out of his dejection. "I turn from you, and listen to the wind, / Which long has raved unnoticed." The speaker is now ready to take responsibility, "to receive what we give," to become a better listener of Nature's song. Instead of hearing the "tortured lengthened out" "that lute sent forth," and "the rushing of an host in rout, / With groans, of trampled men, with smarting wounds," he will ignore all such thoughts of his besieged psyche. Thereby, he will end the inner turmoil that produces self-defeating thoughts. "But hush! There is a pause of deepest silence! / . . . It tells another tale, with sounds less deep and loud! / A tale of less affright, / And tempered with delight."

"Dejection: An Ode" ends on a peaceful note. As the speaker gazes on his sleeping lover in **Stanza 8**, we are reminded of the third and last part of the Grecian ode in which the chorus stood still. Although we are not told that the speaker has regained all that he believes he has lost, he does find peace and solace as he contemplates both his lover and the gifts nature has the power to bestow. "Joy lift her spirit, joy attune her voice; / To her may all things live, from pole to pole, / Their life the eddying of her living soul!" There is healing to be had in the quiet contemplation of Nature. ❀

Critical Views on
"Dejection: An Ode"

JOHN SPENCER HILL ON CLASSICAL AND ENGLISH ODE TRADITIONS

[John Spencer Hill is the author of *Infinity, Faith and Time: Christian Humanism and Renaissance Literature* and *John Milton, Poet, Priest and Prophet: A Study of Divine Vocation in Milton's Poetry and Prose.* In the excerpt below from the chapter, "'Dejection: An Ode,'" Hill discusses Coleridge's poem in terms of the classical and English ode traditions, and the delicate balance of formal and informal characteristics in "Dejection."]

According to Samuel Johnson's *Dictionary of the English Language* (1755), 'the ode is either of the greater or less kind. The less is characterised by sweetness and ease; the greater by sublimity, rapture, and quickness of transition.' The distinction that Johnson is making is that between the literary heirs of Horace and those of Pindar. Gilbert Highet distinguishes the two traditions in this way:

> Among the lyricists who follow classical inspiration, consciously or unconsciously, some are descendants of Pindar, some of Horace. The Pindarics admire passion, daring, and extravagance. Horace's followers prefer reflection, moderation, economy. Pindaric odes follow no pre-established routine, but soar and dive and veer as the wind catches their wing. Horatian lyrics work on quiet, short, well-balanced systems. Pindar represents the ideals of aristocracy, careless courage and the generous heart. Horace is a *bourgeois*, prizing thrift, care, caution, the virtue of self-control. Even the music we can hear through the odes of the two poets and their successors is different. Pindar loves the choir, the festival, the many-footed dance. Horace is a solo singer, sitting in a pleasant room or quiet garden with his lyre. ⟨. . .⟩

By 1802 Coleridge had composed a number of odes, ranging from the turgid 'Pindarick' sublime of 'Ode to the Departing Year' (1796) to the meditative Horatian accents of 'Ode to Tranquillity,' which appeared in the *Morning Post* of 4 December 1801. From its first publication in October 1802, Coleridge called his 'Dejection' an ode. It is, like Wordsworth's 'Ode: Intimations of Immortality', an irregular English Pindaric. And yet it has always existed somewhat uneasily within the confines of this generic description. On the one hand, it is one of the most regular odes in the language: 'five-sixths of its lines', as John Jump has pointed out, 'are either iambic pentameters or alexandrines, nearly four-fifths of them iambic pentameters'. In addition, it shares a significant number of characteristics with Coleridge's Conversation Poems; and some critics—notably G. M. Harper and (with reservations) George Watson—are inclined to group it generically with these earlier poems, while M. H. Abrams (imitating the Augustan distinction between 'greater' and 'lesser' odes) prefers to assign both the best of the Conversation Poems and 'Dejection: An Ode' to a new lyric category which he denominates 'the greater Romantic lyric'. On the other hand, however, there is the fact that Coleridge persistently referred to 'Dejection' as an ode and the fact that the poem is (despite other influences) recognisably part of the English Pindaric tradition. While no one, I think, would deny that Coleridge's 'conversational' mode has left its mark on the poem and is largely responsible for its being so different in many ways from earlier Pindarics in English, it is equally apparent that 'Dejection: An Ode' cannot properly be called a Conversation Poem. Its tone, for one thing, while genial and (at least superficially) familiar, is not intimate and is exalted and dignified to a degree that has no parallel in the Conversation Poems of 1795–8. Its form and style, moreover, are radically unlike those of the earlier poems: it is divided into formal stanzas rather than into apparently artless verse-paragraphs; and, while iambic pentameter provides the prosodic base, there is no blank verse in the poem at all—rhyme is employed throughout and line-lengths are varied. In short, 'Dejection: An Ode' is a sort of middle thing between a traditional Pindaric and a Coleridgean Conversation Poem; and I would agree with A. H. Fairbanks that the poem 'has fair claim to status as the first distinctively Romantic ode'—a status achieved by the 'synthesis of the magnitude and dynamics of the ode with the personal style and immediacy of the conversation poem'.

'Dejection: An Ode' is a poem of paradox, of balanced opposites—the formal and the informal, imaginative loss and imaginative power—held in delicate equilibrium. The magnificent opening stanza (lines 1–20), which merits citation in full, subtly establishes the antitheses that the poem develops as it progresses:

Well! If the Bard was weather-wise, who made
　The grand old ballad of Sir Patrick Spence,
　This night, so tranquil now, will not go hence
Unroused by winds, that ply a busier trade
Than those which mould yon cloud in lazy flakes,
Or the dull sobbing draft, that moans and rakes
Upon the strings of this Æolian lute,
　　Which better far were mute.
　For lo! the New-moon winter-bright!
　And overspread with phantom light,
　(With swimming phantom light o'erspread
　But rimmed and circled by a silver thread)
I see the old Moon, in her lap, foretelling
　The coming-on of rain and squally blast.
And oh! that even now the gust were swelling,
　And the slant night-shower driving loud and fast!
Those sounds which oft have raised me, whilst they awed,
　　And sent my soul abroad,
Might now perhaps their wonted impulse give,
Might startle this dull pain, and make it move and live!

These lines, relaxed and colloquial, giving a sense of ambling, meandering thought, are unobtrusively but firmly controlled by a formal rhyme-scheme that never threatens or interferes with the illusion of genial spontaneity. The formality of rhyme and stanza-form are modulated by an abundance of enjambment and by varied metrical patterns that imitate the ebb and flow of thought and of the rising and falling breeze. The imagery, too, moves effortlessly from the external world to the internal demesne of the poet's mind, blending outness with inscape: the lute, for example, is both an actual Aeolian harp and a metaphor of mind, and the rising wind is both real and a symbol of inspiration. And there is in this stanza, as William Walsh points out, 'a constant transition from particular to general and from general to particular: reflection feeds on the concrete and the concrete holds within it the impulse of the general'. Thus, the moon, while mysteriously overspread with a vague 'phantom light', is yet defined with mathematical precision as 'rimmed and circled by a silver thread'. The surety of the present moment and the present scene are counterbalanced by contingency and a deep-set apprehension of what the future holds; the rising wind, while invoked, is yet feared— for it strikes a deeper chord that reverberates through the stanza from the ominous prolepsis of the epigraph:

And I fear, I fear, my Master dear!
We shall have a deadly storm.

Will the wind, when it comes, be creative or destructive? And the moon, too—the new moon with the old moon in her arms—is similarly ambiguous: does it signify rebirth or death, what is yet to come or what has passed away? Poised between expectation and foreboding, between vivid awareness of the world and an apathetic inability to respond to it, the opening stanza establishes the paradoxes which the following stanzas will explore.

> —John Spencer Hill, *A Coleridge Companion: An Introduction to the Major Poems and the* Biographia Literaria (New York: Macmillan Publishing Company, 1984): pp. 198–201.

HAROLD BLOOM ON CONTINUITY IN THE POEM

[Harold Bloom is an eminent scholar and has written extensively on all the Romantic poets. His books include *The Ringers in the Tower: Studies in the Romantic Tradition* (1971), *The Anxiety of Influence: The Theory of Poetry* (1975) and *Ruin the Sacred Truths: Poetry and Belief from the Bible to the Present* (1989). In the excerpt below from a chapter on Samuel Taylor Coleridge, Bloom argues for a continuity in "Dejection: An Ode" based on an irreversible human process that accepts the permanent loss of imaginative powers, implicitly confirmed by nature.]

There is only one voice in *Dejection: An Ode*. In this poem Coleridge does not argue with himself, though he has need to do so. But the voice is turned against itself with an intensity that only the greatest poets have been able to bring over into language. The ode's continuity as argument presents no problems; *Dejection* overtly rejects the dialectic of Wordsworth's memory-as-salvation. The logic of *Dejection* is that human process is irreversible: imaginative loss is permanent, and nature intimates to us our own mortality always.

The puzzle of *Dejection* is why and how it rejects *as imaginative argument* the Wordsworthian myth. The myth was initially a Coleridgean creation, in the "conversation poems" of 1795–1798, where it is beautifully stated, though always with misgivings. The "why" of rejection belongs to a study of how Coleridge's poetry itself discourses on poetic limits. The "how" is a lesson in the Romantic uses of self-directed argument.

The epigraph to Wordsworth's *Intimations* ode is a motto of natural piety. Against its rainbow Coleridge sets the natural emblem most in opposition: the new moon, with the old moon in its arms. In *Dejection* the storm is predicted, comes on, and finally is "but a mountain-birth," sudden and soon over. The poem's new moon is the Wordsworth surrogate, "Dear Lady! friend devoutest of my choice"; its old moon, Coleridge himself. The principal difference, then, between the two odes is that Wordsworth uses one protagonist passing through several states of being while Coleridge undertakes the lesser imaginative task and risks pathos by doubling the human element yet keeping the voice single. The poem's speaker is doomed to imaginative death; all hope for joy devolves upon the "Lady."

By evading individual progression-through-contraries, Coleridge has no ostensible need for poetic logic. But this evasion could not in itself make a poem of any value; flat personal despair joined to altruism and benevolence is hardly a formula for poetic power. *Dejection* is imaginatively impressive because Coleridge does not succeed in altogether distinguishing himself from the Lady whose joy he celebrates. The curious and yet extraordinarily successful effect is like that of a saint seeking to disavow Christian doctrine by avowing its efficacy for others, less sinful than himself.

Study of *Dejection: An Ode* can well begin backwards, with a consideration of the lines that enable the poem to end on the word "rejoice":

> To her may all things live, from pole to pole,
> Their life the eddying of her living soul!

The image of the eddy is the summary figure of the poem: the flux of nature throughout has prepared for it. Joy, as the effluence of Life, overflows as sound, light, cloud, shower; as a composite luminous and melodic mist of the soul; now solid, now liquid, now vaporous, now pure light or pure sound. This is repetitious summary, but the poem's repetitiveness is meaningful here. The myth of Wordsworth's Child is being rejected; the glory comes and goes, without relation to infancy, childhood, youth, maturity. The progression is simply linear and it is irreversible:

There was a time when, though my path was rough,
    This joy within me dallied with distress,
And all misfortunes were but as the stuff
    Whence Fancy made me dreams of happiness:
For hope grew round me, like the twining vine,
And fruits, and foliage, not my own, seemed mine.
But now afflictions bow me down to earth.

The eddy has stopped its pole-to-pole movement; the cycle of joy is over. Taken literally, Coleridge's myth of dejection is a bizarre reinforcement of a single stage in the poetic argument of *Resolution and Independence*:

We poets in our youth begin in gladness,
But thereof comes in the end despondency and madness.

If *Dejection* had only its Stanzas I to VI and its climactic in Stanza VIII, it could not be defended from the charge of pathos. The usually evaded Stanza VII, which is generally considered a transitional mood piece, controls the poem's logic and equips it to avoid self-indulgence. The structure of the poem is in two units: Stanzas I, VII, VIII, and Stanzas II–VI. The first group are respectively devoted to the pre-storm calm, the storm itself, and the subsequent calm, which is analogous to the peace at the end of a formalized tragedy. The middle stanzas are argument, between Coleridge-as-Wordsworthian and Coleridge-in-dejection, with the latter dialectically triumphant. The connecting unit between the groups opens Stanza VII, in which the "viper thoughts" of II-VI are dismissed as "Reality's dark dream":

I turn from you, and listen to the wind,
    Which long has raved unnoticed.

As he listens to the wind, he resolves his poem. The resolution is purely dialectical in that the stanza offers a set of assumptions that *include* the opposing Wordsworthian and Coleridgean views on the relationship between external nature and the poet's creative joy. Certainly the resolution is indirect, and perhaps too ingenious. But the curious seventh stanza cannot be ignored as an embarrassing digression; it is the crisis of the poem, akin to the silence between the eighth and ninth stanzas of the *Intimations* ode. There the dialectic rises to poetic finality because it is a dialectic of discourse itself. The conflict of discourse and silence is resolved in favor of silence, with the result that the discourse, when it begins again, can move in reverse and state the contrary of the preceding stanzas.

—Harold Bloom, *The Visionary Company: A Reading of English Romantic Poetry* (Ithaca, N.Y.: Cornell University Press, 1961): pp. 222–24.

Reeve Parker on the Poem's Formal Elements in Relation to Its Intention

[Reeve Parker is one of the editors of *The Triumph of Style: Modes of Non-Fiction*. In the excerpt below from the chapter, "'Dejection: An Ode,'" Parker discusses the final version of the poem (published on Wordsworth's wedding day) in terms of the relationship between formal elements and intention.]

The goal of my reading in this chapter is to describe and interpret in the final version of "Dejection: An Ode" what Coleridge might have called the order of imitation—in other words to arrive at some description of the "general" and "universal" in the poem—and thus to argue that the poem was not merely the result of a purging of emotion in the interests of discretion. To deplore, for the sake of confessional sincerity, the imposition of form as a falsifying of actual behavior and experience is to misconstrue the processes of conscious (and unconscious) self-expression. In the preface to his 1796 *Poems* Coleridge argued for a salutary egotism in poetic composition, contending that "the communicativeness of our nature leads us to describe our sorrows" and that from this exerted intellectual activity "a pleasure results which is gradually associated and mingles as a corrective with the painful subject of the description." As we have seen, Coleridge thought that such egotistic conversation could be heuristic, especially in the heightened order of verse, and that the discovery toward which the poet won his difficult way was not only intellectual comprehension of the distress but also release of the mind's processive energies, the life that opposed the death-in-life of melancholy solipsism. About a year after publishing "Dejection: An Ode" in the *Morning Post*, Coleridge explored the old ground of his 1796 preface in a notebook entry that has the excitement of fresh recognition: "One excellent use of communication of Sorrows to a Friend is this: that in relating what ails us we ourselves first know exactly what the real Grief is—& see it for itself, in its own form & limits. Unspoken Grief is a misty medley, of which the real affliction only plays the first fiddle—blows the horn, to a scattered mob of obscure feelings." Though the remark emphasizes how communication leads one to articulate and focus what is otherwise scattered and dim, when it is read in conjunction with another notebook entry almost immediately following, we can see that Coleridge is also centrally concerned with the pleasurable activity resulting from such effort at meditative consciousness. Analysis and creative release work hand in hand to alleviate the initial wretchedness:

> Some painful Feeling, bodily or of the mind / some form or feeling has recalled a past misery to the Feeling, & not to the conscious memory—I brood over what has befallen of evil / what is the worst that could befall me? What is that Blessing which is most present & perpetual to my Fancy and Yearnings? Sara! Sara!—The Loss then of this first bodies itself out to me / —& if I have not heard from you very recently, & if the last letter had not happened to be full of explicit Love & Feeling, then I conjure up Shadows into Substances—& am miserable / Misery conjures up other Forms, & binds them into Tales & Events—activity is always Pleasure—the Tale grows pleasanter—& at length you come to me / you are by my bed side, in some lonely Inn, where I lie deserted—there you have found me—there you are weeping over me!—Dear, dear, Woman! ⟨. . .⟩

As in "Frost at Midnight," in "Dejection: An Ode" the progress enacted is from voicing distress, by uneasy and fanciful toying with a superstitious belief, to discerning how the terms of that superstition and the imagery associated with them can sustain a different and more substantial creed. In no other meditative poem besides "Frost at Midnight" does imagery concerned with the eddying energies of the natural world work with more subtle or ingenious cogency. That imagery and what has, somewhat misleadingly, been called the controlling metaphor of the poem— the storm—warrant close attention.

The most remarkable image is, certainly, that of the moon in the opening stanza:

> Well! If the Bard was weather-wise, who made
> The grand old ballad of Sir Patrick Spence,
> This night, so tranquil now, will not go hence
> Unroused by winds, that ply a busier trade
> Than those which mould yon cloud in lazy flakes,
> Or the dull sobbing draft, that moans and rakes
> Upon the strings of this Æolian lute,
> Which better far were mute. ⟨...⟩

Coleridge's attention, both here and in the epigraph from the "Ballad of Sir Patrick Spence," to the lore of superstition introduces a mood of uneasy reflection (like that at the opening of "Frost at Midnight" or "This Lime-Tree Bower My Prison") in words that, as Donald Davie has observed, "slide down a long scale of emotion from something not far short of geniality to a desperate melancholy."

—Reeve Parker, *Coleridge's Meditative Art* (Ithaca, N.Y.: Cornell University Press, 1975): pp. 181–184.

SUSAN MILITZER LUTHER ON INTERPRETING THE POEM

[Susan Militzer Luther is the author of *Christabel as Dream Reverie* (1976). In this excerpt, Luther discusses a little-known Coleridge poem entitled "The Garden of Boccaccio" and explains its usefulness in interpreting "Dejection: An Ode."]

In *The Dark Night of Samuel Taylor Coleridge* (1960) Marshall Suther praises "The Garden of Boccaccio" as "Coleridge's version of 'Sailing to Byzantium'"; and in *Visions of Xanadu* (1965) Suther goes so far as to call it "the last real poem [Coleridge] wrote." ⟨In *Coleridge the Poet* (1966)⟩ George Watson even more resoundingly asserts that the poem "ought to be better known; it ought, in fact, to be the poem first turned to, after the conversation poems, the 'Mariner', 'Kubla Khan' and 'Christabel', to confirm the stature of [Coleridge's] poetic art." Yet "The Garden of Boccaccio" has still been virtually erased from most surveys of the Coleridgean landscape. ⟨...⟩

Written in 1828, the poem was first published in *The Keepsake* for 1829, an annual "*Gaudy Book*," as Coleridge called it in a letter to Alaric Watts. A poem-about-a-picture, "The Garden of Boccaccio" at first sight appears to be little more than an appreciation of its companion illustration, an engraving of Thomas Stothard's depiction of the garden to which Neifile leads her companions on the Third Day of the *Decameron*. Given its self-proclaimed allegiance to "fancy," its heroic couplets, its occasionally coy, archaic diction and its tincture of "romance," "The Garden of Boccaccio" does in a way seem precious, no more than an "exquisite design" or topiary-piece straight out of the land of "faery" evoked by the volume in which it first appeared.

Coleridge himself expressed the rather modest hope that readers such as Watts might find it "a vigorous *Copy of Verses*." One presumes that Coleridge meant "set" of verses, "modeled after" Stothard's drawing; but the term "*Copy*" hints at the poem's place in a larger, reproductive design. It appears again in the collective editions of 1829 and 1834, where it immediately follows "The Improvisatore," there titled "New Thoughts on Old Subjects." And "The Garden of Boccaccio" itself, as George Whalley and George Ridenour some time ago pointed out, is a late response to, or elaboration of, themes central in canonical poems, especially "Dejection: An Ode." Not simply imitative, echoic or allusive, the poem contains an element of self-parody, enacting what Linda Hutcheon calls "a stylistic confrontation, a modern recoding which establishes difference at the heart of similarity."

This "difference at the heart of similarity" appears in the poem's first lines, when the poet-narrator explains that,

> Of late, in one of those most weary hours,
> When life seems emptied of all genial powers,
> A dreary mood, which he who ne'er has known
> May bless his happy lot, I sate alone;
> And, from the numbing spell to win relief,
> Call'd on the PAST for thought of glee or grief.
> In vain! bereft alike of grief and glee,
> I sate and cow'r'd o'er my own vacancy!
> And as I watch'd the dull continuous ache,
> Which, all else slumb'ring, seem'd alone to wake;
> O Friend! long wont to notice yet conceal,
> And soothe by silence what words cannot heal,

I but half saw that quiet hand of thine
Place on my desk this exquisite design,
Boccaccio's Garden and its faery,
The love, the joyaunce, and the gallantry!
An IDYLL, with Boccaccio's spirit warm,
Framed in the silent poesy of form.

His "dreary mood" recalls the "wan and heartless mood" of "Dejection," while the "dull continuous ache" points backward to the "dull pain" and its avatar, the "dull sobbing draft" which sounds the strings of the aeolian harp. In "The Garden of Boccaccio" the narrator describes one of those times when "life seems emptied of all genial powers"; in "Dejection" the speaker's "genial spirits fail." Further, the appeal to "joyaunce" in "The Garden of Boccaccio" evokes not only the many references to "joy" and (though fewer) to "joyance" throughout Coleridge's poems, but the impassioned paean to Joy in strophe V of the ode. Both works describe a lack of animation, a state of spiritual and emotional "vacancy," a "void" which "relief" cannot enter, proscribed by the "numbing spell." "The Garden of Boccaccio"'s transformation of the ode's failing "genial *spirits*" into "genial *powers*" which seem to have been "emptied" from the vessel of life brings to the surface the connection with "genius" latent, as Paul Magnuson points out, in the earlier phrase, making it clear that here, too, *anima*, the poet's "shaping spirit," not simply lack of "mirth," is at stake. In a further absorption of the personal elements of the earlier poem (and the verse-letter which preceded it) into the *topos* of vocation, "The Garden of Boccaccio" dissolves the earlier addressees into multiples of the Muse: "Sara" and the "Lady" of verse-letter and ode become a non-gendered "Friend" (Anne Gillman, though the text does not identify her) and the muse-maidens of picture and "mazy page." "Edmund," the addressee of the first published version of "Dejection," a name substituted for "Wordsworth," divides into the "gentle artist" Stothard and Boccaccio himself. But the elaborative shrinking of Joy into "joyaunce" (the only instance of this spelling in Coleridge's poems) indicates how far "The Garden of Boccaccio" has come from its predecessor's dark intensity of feeling as well as of generic ambition. The insertion of the *u* into a term which already marks itself as belonging to myth and "romance" underscores the poem's artificiality, its remoteness from "life" and its identity as a made thing rather than a serious, straightforward outpouring of "the passion and the life, whose fountains are within."

This change in emphasis does not simply represent an icefall, however. The poem's substitution of the figure of form—"the silent poesy of form"—for the figure of voice resolves in *muta poesis* the split "voice" of "Dejection" and critiques the naive egotism of the trope, or myth, of self-originating voice. That is, the trope *of* form undercuts some of the pretensions of the ode *as* form. Paul Fry suggests that "the aim of the ode is to recover and usurp the voice to which hymns defer: not merely to participate in the presence of voice but to *be* the voice." The poem-about-a-picture, or *ekphrasis*, on the other hand, is more modest in its usurpations. It unabashedly eschews originality and singularity to explore the originary power of elaboration, of secondariness.

—Susan Militzer Luther, "The Lost Garden of Coleridge," *The Wordsworth Circle* 22, no. 1 (Winter 1991): pp. 24–25.

TILOTTAMA RAJAN ON THE POEM'S AMBIGUITY

> [Tilottama Rajan is the author of *The Supplement of Reading: Figures of Understanding in Romantic Theory* and a contributing editor of *Romanticism, History and the Possibility of Genre: Reforming Literature 1789–1837*. In the excerpt below from the chapter "Image and Reality in Coleridge's Lyric Poetry," Rajan discusses the interpretational ambiguities in "Dejection: An Ode." She attributes these to the equivocal evidence of whether the speaker has solved his crisis, namely whether he has found unity between nature and his own newly-restored imaginative powers.]

One of the central ambiguities in "Dejection: An Ode" arises from an uncertainty about whether epiphany is created by a cooperation between the light reflected and the light bestowed, or by a projection of light from within. The crisis of the poem arises precisely from a failure in mediation: the failure of the landscape, whose beauty is only the calm before the storm, to provide for the poet's feelings an outward language that is continuous rather than intermittent. What is apparent in the poem is that all seasons are not sweet, as Coleridge had once claimed. Thus the poet seeks to separate himself from nature, to take onto himself the blame for his dejection in order to reclaim the initiative of renewed vision. In the concluding celebration of Asra he claims for imagination the power to transcend distance and sterility, and to represent an ideal that is absent through an act of unmediated vision. Such vision is purely inward, liberated from the need for physical perception, and therefore from the reality which might confirm it but might also expose it.

It is often observed that the paradox of this poem lies in Coleridge's ability to create despite his professed inability to do so. But in fact almost the reverse is true. The dilemma of the poem is that there is no consolation in the power of imagination to constitute an ideal that is not fulfilled in the prose of the world. The poet is able to "give" life to Asra, but does not receive it back into the creating self, which remains estranged from the radical innocence that it projects. The existence of this dejected self constitutes a denial of the "life" given by it, and constantly exposes the ideal as illusory from the vantage point of the real. Precisely because he has liberated the imaginary from the real, the poet has made impossible the remarriage of vision and actuality demanded by the mediatory assumptions of the conversation mode, if not by poetry itself as a communicative mode. Or, to put it differently, such mediation is achievable only at the cost of reimplicating the desire for the imaginary in the knowledge of the real.

"Dejection" goes considerably further than other poems in recognizing the impotence of radical idealism: in recognizing, with Hegel, that the act of envisioning a nonexistent ideal is, in its very nature, "a dual state of mind" rather than a liberating act. Other Romantics tacitly admit this linkage between desire and knowledge in imaging hope and despair as twins rather than antitheses, as shadow and substance or concave and convex. To imagine an ideal that existed in an autonomous realm of illusion would be to imagine that impossible phenomenon which Sartre calls a "shut imaginary consciousness." Such a consciousness is completely unconscious of anything outside itself, and is therefore without "being-in-the-world." Because it exists in a purely imaginary world turned in on itself through dream, death, or fiction, without any conception of reality, it is closed to the insight that might perceive it as illusory. But what is apparent in a poem such as "Dejection," and more explicitly in the late poems, is that there is no such state of consciousness. The imagination can construct an ideal that does not exist, but it must then deconstruct this ideal from the vantage point of existence. A poem either accepts this deconstructive potential within imagination or condemns itself to be a self-frustrated literary structure, which projects within itself aesthetic norms that are discontinuous with the experience it dramatizes.

—Tilottama Rajan, *Dark Interpreter: The Discourse of Romanticism* (Ithaca, N.Y.: Cornell University Press, 1980): pp. 250–252.

Thematic Analysis of
"Kubla Khan"

Published in May 1816, the composition date of this enigmatic poem has been much debated, ranging from the summer of 1797 to the spring of 1800; the fall of 1797, however, is generally accepted as the date of composition. In the preface of the poem, the poet indicates he had written the poem during the summer of 1797 under conditions he clearly delineates. According to Coleridge, he was living in a "lonely farmhouse between Porlock and Linton" and "ill in health," had fallen asleep in his chair while reading about the historical Kubla Khan, founder of the 13th-century Mongol dynasty in China, in Purchas' *Pilgrimage*, written in 1613. Coleridge tells us he dreamt of all the luxurious images depicted in Purchas, of "pleasant Springs, delightfull Streames . . . and in the middest thereof a sumptuous house of pleasure, which may be removed from place to place." Upon awakening, with pen and paper in hand in order to record his dream, Coleridge was interrupted by a visitor from Porlock and detained for over an hour, so that when the stranger left, Coleridge's recollection of his vision had all but disappeared. To express the lost vision, Coleridge includes some lines from *The Picture; or the Lover's Resolution*: "Then all the charm / Is broken—all that phantom world so fair / Vanishes, and a thousand circlets spread, . . . Stay awhile, / Poor youth! . . . The visions will return!" All he can do now is offer the reader a fragment of the account he intended, "describing with equal fidelity the dream of pain and disease." That fragment is the poem, "Kubla Khan." The poem can be read as an interpretation of the poetic process itself, in which the power of creativity is at war with the poet's anxiety that he is too late, that other poets have already said the same thing.

From the first two lines of the **first stanza**, Khan is portrayed as a ruler in complete control over his domain, not unlike an artist who believes in the strength of his own creative power. Khan has full legal authority to command the construction of his own palace: "In Xanadu did Kubla Khan / A stately pleasure dome decree." The rest of this first stanza is a lush description of the landscape in Xanadu, yet at the same time the stanza contains intense images of enclosure, defensiveness, and the need to protect this world from outside intrusion. The luxurious construction seems to be inaccessible to mere mortals. However, here the poet may abide in a world arranged by his own fancy; he has gained access to this otherwise inaccessible world through the power of imagination. "Where Alph, the sacred river ran / Through caverns measureless to man / Down to a sunless sea. / So twice five miles of fertile ground / With walls and towers were girdled round." Whether we read the poem from the point of view of Khan the ruler, or from the perspective of the triumphant poetic voice, this imaginative space is full of tension, anxiety, and the fear of invasion (either by the outside world or by the spirit of poetic forebears who have already had the final word). Thus, Xanadu begins to emerge as a fortress, or perhaps even as a prison for those who reside within its inviolable walls. "So twice five miles of fertile ground, / With walls and towers were girdled round." Above all else, however, Coleridge sets forth the dynamics of poetic competition: he will compete with Khan to construct a far lovelier paradise than the one of which he has just read.

In the **second stanza**, the "incense-bearing tree" and "sunny spots of greenery" of the first stanza are transformed into a frightening terrain, "[a] savage place! as holy and enchanted / As e'er beneath a waning moon was haunted." This stanza bears many resemblances to the world of medieval romance. First, the enchanted forest, with all its magic and danger, is an important topos in the Arthurian legend. Furthermore, the waning moon has always been a powerful symbol of femininity, and is yet another version of the "woman wailing for her demon lover."

The presence of these two images have profound consequences for our interpretation of the poem. To begin with, the moon, which presides over nature and affects the ebb and tide of the ocean, is here "waning." This image of fading power describes far more than just the night; it also makes a statement about the diminution of creative potency. With respect to the wailing woman, the inclusion of this element of medieval romance becomes a strong statement that the woman's chances of being united with her lover are hopeless, for the medieval romantic convention mandates that love must be forever unrequited in order to perpetuate the relentless quest for fulfillment.

These images of suspended animation/imagination are the poet's worst nightmare; he fears his creativity has come to an end. Furthermore, just as this nightmare rings the poetic death knell, a violent upheaval occurs and all hope collapses. "A mighty fountain momently was forced: amid whose swift half-intermitted burst / Huge fragments vaulted like rebounding hail."

Finally, there is also a Chaucerian (and therefore medieval) allusion to the garrulous eagle who advises the poet, Geoffrey Chaucer, to ignore the chaff and write of the corn, to get rid of the debris left by the thresher, the "chaffy grain" (here, the poetic predecessor) and write of the kernel or essential vision of poetic truth. And so the stanza ends with "[a]ncestral voices prophesying war! / The shadow of the dome of pleasure / Floated midway on the waves." If the poem is read as a "tour" through the often treacherous, yet thrilling and fantastic realm of the imagination, then the poetic predecessors have returned to compete with the living poet.

The **third stanza** concerns Coleridge's vision of the Abyssinian maid. Critics have debated whether this last stanza is connected to the other two—or if in fact this second vision is merely a fragment of another poem. If the poet intended it to be understood as a new vision, then its primary distinction from the "dream vision" of the pleasure dome is that the poet is now fully awake and conscious. The vision is born out of the great cataclysm of the preceding stanza in which "the dome of pleasure" has sunk "in tumult to a lifeless ocean." The sensual effects of this newly-created paradise are far more aural than visual, and the sounds that emanate from the dulcimer are much softer and very different from the sounds of the fountain in the second stanza, "[a]mid whose swift half-intermitted burst / Huge fragments vaulted like rebounding hail." Indeed, the dulcimer's music is nothing less than a "symphony." Most significantly, the Abyssinian maid sings of Mount Abora, an allusion to Book IV of *Paradise Lost*. The poet is acknowledging both his wish to follow in Milton's footsteps and his fear that it may not be possible, for Coleridge posits that thought as desire rather than an absolute certainty: "Could I revive within me / Her symphony and song / . . . I would build that dome in air." The poet ends on an ambiguous note, his work a fragment of creative imagination that reaches no final conclusion. ✿

Critical Views on
"Kubla Khan"

ANTHONY JOHN HARDING ON COLERIDGE'S
MYTHMAKING

[Anthony John Harding is the author of *The Reception of Myth in English Romanticism* and *Milton, the Metaphysicals and Romanticism*. In the excerpt below from the chapter entitled "Beyond Mythology," Harding discusses "Kubla Khan" in the context of Coleridge's mythmaking. Coleridge's creation of an ambiguous landscape, the core of which can be located in the Christian tradition, Harding sees as an attempt to break down the barriers between the sacred and the profane.]

The Mariner's emergence into the post-mythological era has been a traumatic one, and his psychic scars remain with him. Though he has unselfconsciously created the mythology which brought him self-knowledge and a degree of freedom, he is not yet master of it. He remains the unwilling object of daemonic possession, . . . limping along the road to the Enlightenment vision of perfected humanity.

"Kubla Khan" presents us with a similarly ambivalent portrait. The first thirty-six lines of the poem encapsulate the mythic constructs of the Orient: neither haphazard antiquarianism nor an unprecedented attack of the collective unconscious can be credited with responsibility for this narrative. After Elinor Shaffer's lucid demonstration of the ferment of syncretistic thought that lay behind "Kubla Khan," it should no longer be possible to take seriously explanations of the poem based on pathology or associative psychology; nor, more important still, should we continue to refer to Coleridge's mind as consisting of a pagan half which possessed all the creativity and a Christian half which acted as his "orthodox censor."

As a Christian in an age which already stood outside mythology, which looked back on it as on a road previously travelled (or, to use Campbell's metaphor, as the womb from which it had emerged), Coleridge understood that the poet's task must now be to survey mythology from above: to claim it as a dynamic heritage, not as the exhausted fictions derided by Voltaire. "Coleridge's transcendental enterprise was to lay bare the source of mythology, the sense for a God in the human race."

While Shaffer is surely right to summarize in this way the impulse from which "Kubla Khan" sprang, we have to recognize that her work has raised in acute form all the problems associated with demythologization and its close relative in literary criticism, secularization. Modern humanistic scholarship sometimes tends to overlook the fact that at the very centre of Christian tradition lies the most potent of all images for the overthrow of hieratic religion and the release of the sacred into common experience: the rending of the veil of the temple. For the Christian poet there are grounds for believing that any barriers which once existed between the sacred and the profane have been thrown down. The Atonement or reuniting (at-one-ment) of God and humankind implies that (in Frye's words) "a channel of communication between the divine and human is now open." Yet such a statement at once involves the recollection of a historical event—and therefore of the poet's own position in historical time, his fallibility and his finitude. A disturbing infiltration of the anagogical into the historical, thoughts of the end of all things into the image of an existing realized perfection, is an undeniable feature of "Kubla Khan," as it is of the thirteenth chapter of *Biographia Literaria,* in which the primary Imagination is held to be a repetition, in the finite mind, of the eternal, divine act of creation and is echoed by the secondary Imagination or poetic power, which coexists with the conscious will. Here, too, the process of recreating and unifying sometimes appears to be threatened by a counter-tendency within the secondary Imagination itself towards dissolution: "It dissolves, diffuses, dissipates, in order to recreate; or where this process is rendered impossible, yet still at all events it struggles to idealize and to unify."

Lawrence Kramer notes the same pattern of dissolution followed by recreation in "Kubla Khan": the woman wailing for her demon-lover, for erotic possession by an unknown primal other, and who thus personifies the "daemonic" aspect of Coleridgean imagination, is transmuted and taken up into the healing, idealized figure of the Abyssinian maid. Kramer's purpose in pointing out the similarity is "to link the daemonic imagination . . . with the romantic imagination of the *Biographia Literaria*," arguing the "the daemonic, in Romantic poems, rarely appears without generating a later appearance of its romantic contrary, which then proceeds to transcend, transform, or evade the daemonic vision."

—Anthony John Harding, *Coleridge and the Inspired Word* (Montreal: McGill-Queen's University Press, 1985): pp. 50–52.

CARL R. WOODRING ON THE POEM'S POLITICAL CONTEXT

[Carl R. Woodring is a well-known scholar and has written several books on the Romantic and Victorian periods. His books include *Politics in English Romantic Poetry* (1970) and *Nature Into Art: Cultural Transformations in Nineteenth-Century Britain* (1989). In the excerpt below from his 1961 book *Politics in the Poetry of Coleridge*, Woodring, citing both historical and biographical facts, discusses the political context of "Kubla Khan," suggesting that the poem can be interpreted as an expression of Coleridge's distaste for luxury and political ambition.]

His distaste for the luxury and ambition of princes may help to explain *Kubla Khan*. He has clearly erected in that poem an antithesis between the measured and the measureless, the sunny and the sunless, the pleasure-dome and the deep romantic chasm, the pleasurable and the sacred, the decree of Kubla Khan and the prophecy amid tumult. Kubla said, Let there be a dome, and there was a dome. "But oh!" he heard from far "Ancestral voices prophesying war!" Setting aside the poles of drunken and sober Freudianism, critical analyses of the poem divide basically over attitudes toward the eastern potentate. Is the poem for Kubla or against him? Or, as possible but unlikely, does it lean neither for nor against? We need to resolve this point before we can declare Kubla the symbol of a poet decreeing the thing of beauty in his imagination, instead of a temporal lord creating in a mode less durable than the poet's mode opposed to it. Coleridge certainly in 1796, and almost certainly in 1798 or 1799, would have been against

Kubla's presumption. If he associated the dome of his poem with wealth and pleasure, as well as with a potentate, he would condemn the dome rather than the supernatural forces that threaten it. Purchas, his most immediate source, called it "a sumptuous house of pleasure." By the term "a Pleasure house," in a letter of May, 1799, to Thomas Poole, Coleridge refers to some kind of love-nest where a German subaltern killed his mistress and then himself. To arrive at this nest, the officer "made a pleasure party in a Sledge with a woman with whom he lived in criminal connection." The German account that Coleridge seems to be summarizing contains no direct suggestion of either a "pleasure party" or a "Pleasure house." It is an odd coincidence, if it is nothing more, that Leigh Hunt thought he remembered a variation of the opening lines of the poem in which Kubla Khan did "A stately *pleasure-house ordain.*"

Catherine herself may hover malignly near. Kubla's "sunny pleasure-dome with caves of ice" may possibly not be constructed even partly of ice; its glamor may be enhanced merely by proximity to natural "caves of ice." But the "bubble of ice" in Cashmere, noted by Coleridge for use in his proposed hymn to the moon and considered by J. L. Lowes a direct source for *Kubla Khan*, is no nearer to the dome and its setting in the poem than a pleasure-dome, itself of ice, decreed in a despotic whim by Empress Anna, a notable predecessor of Catherine, shortly before her death in 1740. Her ice-palace, "stately" in its perverse way, may have had a strong influence on the poem. It was "the work of man," admired, unnatural, and unworthy, as William Cowper described and condemned it for his contemporaries—and Coleridge's—in Book V of *The Task*. Cannons of ice had fired metal balls when the Empress forced a courtier in disfavor to marry and to display himself with his ugly bride naked on a bed of ice in the mock-palace. English interest in these cold games began about 1770, when Hume edited a translation of General Manstein's *Memoirs of Russia*. In 1778 John Glen King published *A Letter to . . . the Lord Bishop of Durham . . . With a View of the Flying Mountains of Zarsko Sello near St. Petersbourg*, including a fold-out illustration of the pleasurable device of "flying mountains": over artificial mounds of snow, each hollowed for a grotto, the Empress Elizabeth and her guests (and later Catherine and hers) rode in elaborate toboggans, which a machine worked by horses then drew to the pleasure-hut on the highest mound, in preparation for the next gay adventure. Naturally the almost iceless English were impressed.

Coleridge could not have failed to know of the Empress' ice-palace, however incorrectly he may have remembered for the *Biographia Literaria* that he had made a contumelious reference to it in an essay of 1793: "During my first Cambridge vacation, I assisted a friend in a contribution for a literary society in Devonshire: and in this I remember to have compared Darwin's work to the Russian palace of ice, glittering, cold and transitory." In the agony of his love for Sara Hutchinson, perhaps in 1805, he asked if true love were not of more worth than beauty, wealth, or family. His words are these, in the third stanza of *Separation*:

> Is not true Love of higher price
> > Than outward Form, though fair to see,
> Wealth's glittering fairy-dome of ice,
> > Or echo of proud ancestry?—

> —Carl R. Woodring, *Politics in the Poetry of Coleridge* (Madison: The University of Wisconsin Press, 1961): pp. 49–51.

DAVID PERKINS ON THE UNITY BETWEEN THE PROSE PREFACE AND THE POEM

[David Perkins is a well-known scholar who has written extensively on the Romantic poets. His books include *Wordsworth and the Poetry of Sincerity* and *The Quest for Permanence*. In the excerpt below from his article, "The Imaginative Vision of 'Kubla Khan': On Coleridge's Introductory Note," Perkins discusses the unity between the prose preface and the actual poem, a unity which is often overlooked by other critics. Perkins sees the introductory note as the creation of the first of two myths, the theme of poetic inspiration and its irretrievable loss attributed to the mysterious intruder from Porlock.]

Coleridge's introductory note to *Kubla Khan* weaves together two myths with potent imaginative appeal. The myth of the lost poem tells how an inspired work was mysteriously given to the poet and then dispelled irrecoverably. The nonexistent lines haunt the imagination more than any actual poem could. John Livingston Lowes used to tell his classes, W. Jackson Bate remembers, "If there is any man in the history of literature who should be hanged, drawn, and quartered, it is the man on business from Porlock." ⟨. . .⟩ The note describes the poet as a solitary, a dreamer, and a reader of curious lore, such as *Purchas His Pilgrimage*. He is not portrayed as a habitual taker of drugs but rather the opposite: an "anodyne" had been prescribed for an illness and had the profound effect the note describes because, as the reader is supposed to infer, Coleridge was not used to the drug. But the motif of being drugged is also part of the *symboliste* myth of the poet. Only to a poet of this kind, withdrawn in dreams and uncertain in his inspiration, could the person from Porlock be a serious intrusion. That the man from Porlock comes "on business" is also typical of the *symboliste* ethos, in which ordinary life and "business" were viewed as antithetical to poetry.

How the introductory note should be printed has not been much discussed, but editors have disagreed in practice. In popular anthologies it may be omitted altogether. If it is, the poem may not be read with the assumption that it is unfinished, particularly when, as is generally done, the editor also deletes Coleridge's 1834 subtitle, "Or, A Vision in a Dream. A Fragment." Since in Romantic poetry "Vision," "Dream," and "Fragment" are practically genres, a reader's experience of the poem must be quite different when the expectations evoked by these terms are not activated. ⟨. . .⟩

My purpose in this essay is to inquire what difference it makes. The introductory note guides our reading of the poem from start to finish. Without it, most readers would interpret the poem as asserting the power and potential sublimity of the poet, who can be compared to the great Khan. With the introductory note, this assertion is still present, but it is strongly undercut; the poem becomes richer and more complex, and the theme of lost inspiration is much more heavily weighted. Since many critics have stressed that the introductory note apologizes for the poem and minimizes its significance, there is no need to dwell further on these points. Instead, I shall emphasize that the introductory note gives the poem a plot it would not otherwise have, indicates genres to which the poem belongs, and presents images and themes that interrelate with those in the poem.

In previous articles and books, the only critics who have discussed the problems I take up are Irene H. Chayes, Kathleen M. Wheeler, and Jean-Pierre Mileur. For Chayes, the introductory note is a "literary invention" that "serves as an improvised argument" of the poem; it informs the reader that "the unacknowledged point of view" in the first thirty-six lines of the poem "is that of a man asleep, probably dreaming"; and it offers a "general structural parallel" to the poem, since in both the introductory note and the poem "poetic composition of one kind occurs in the past but in some way is imperfect, and poetic composition of another kind is planned for the future but remains unachieved." Wheeler agrees with Chayes that the introductory note is "a highly literary piece of composition" and that it has thematic similarities to the last eighteen lines of the poem. She thinks that the speaker of the introductory note is not to be taken as Coleridge but as a literal-minded and naive persona whom Coleridge creates "as a model to the reader of how not to respond to the poem." Once the reader recognizes himself in the persona, Wheeler argues, he feels a revulsion and becomes more imaginative and perceptive. Since Coleridge intended all this, his ironic representation of himself in the persona as a "laughing-stock" was "a gesture of incalculable generosity." She arrives at this theory because she wants to make the introductory note analogous to the glosses of the *Ancient Mariner.* Mileur also believes that the introductory note is a "self-conscious fiction" with literary quality. It "constitutes an interpretation of the poem" and itself "cries out for interpretation." He makes specific suggestions to which I am indebted, but his interest is less in the relation of the introductory note to the poem than in general issues this relation poses or illustrates— "immanence" and "presence" versus "revision" and "belatedness."

—David Perkins, "The Imaginative Vision of '*Kubla Khan*': On Coleridge's Introductory Note." In *Coleridge, Keats, and the Imagination: Romanticism and Adam's Dream,* eds. J. Robert Barth, S.J., and John L. Mahoney (Columbia: University of Missouri Press, 1990): pp. 97–99.

CLAIRE MILLER COLOMBO ON POETIC FORM

[Claire Miller Colombo is the author of the article "This
Pen of Mine Will Say Too Much: Public Performance in the
Journals of Anna Larpent." In the excerpt below from her
article "Reading Scripture, Writing Self: Coleridge's
Animation of the 'Dead Letter'" Colombo argues that in
"Kubla Khan" Coleridge seems to have considered poetic
form as derivative of scriptural form. She discusses the
ensuing tensions created by that perspective.]

Like "The Eolian Harp," "Kubla Khan" experiments with imaginative
absolutism. But while the former poem positively affirms the value
of relationality and hope, the latter does so negatively by exploring
the conditions of alienation and fear. "The Eolian Harp"'s economy
of ownership based on exchange is transmuted in "Kubla Khan" into
an economy of ownership based on self-inflation. The final
moments of "The Eolian Harp" find the speaker valuing his
possessions because they have issued from God and will ultimately
return to God: to possess is to anticipate surrender to the
communal. But in "Kubla Khan" the mock-symbolic garden and
pleasure dome, unlike the mock-symbolic harp, are not relinquished
by their owner, Khan. Rather, they are appropriated by the poet-
figure himself, who claims dominion over all dimensions of the
poem—internally, the landscape and the visionary force that shapes
it, and externally, the reader who experiences the poem and must
regard the poet-figure with "holy dread." "The Eolian Harp"'s
anticipated surrender to God is replaced in "Kubla Khan" by the
poet-figure's surrender to self.

Along with "Christabel" (Part I) and "The Ancient Mariner,"
Coleridge creates "Khan" during a period of financial and moral
desperation. In October 1797 he complains that "I suppose that at
last I must become a Unitarian minister as a less evil than
starvation." In early 1798 he is spared this "evil" by accepting the
Wedgwood annuity. Coleridge justifies his ultimate acceptance of the
annuity by regarding the arrangement as a form of exchange; he
writes to Poole in January, 1798 that "I long to be at home with you,
and to settle, and persevere in, some mode of repaying the
Wedgwoods thro' the medium of Mankind." Whether such a
medium of reparation is, as Basil Willey calls it, "high-minded

casuistry" or genuine Christian beneficence is debatable, but Coleridge's acceptance of the offer is clearly motivated by both religious principle and artistic practice. Coleridge first declined the Wedgwoods' offer on the grounds that "I could by means of your kindness subsist for the two next years, & enjoy leisure & external comfort. But anxiety for the future would remain & increase, as it is probable my children will come fast on me." Accepting the second offer may indeed have incited in the poet some degree of guilt, or at least apprehension: indefinite "leisure & external comfort," free of charge, could easily cultivate Khan-like tendencies. Writing the poem, then, may have been for Coleridge a preventive measure; imagining the solipsistic extreme of his new artistic and financial freedom was perhaps negative self-encouragement to "defend that cause to which I have solemnly devoted my best efforts . . . and, as I have received the gospel freely, freely to give it."

If "Kubla Khan" was an exorcism of the version of himself the poet feared—the self that received without giving—it is understandable that the poem remained unpublished until 1816. But why was it published at *that* time? Walter Bate, taking at face value Coleridge's 1816 labeling of the poem as a "psychological curiosity" rather than worthy poetry, casts Coleridge as a poetic weakling motivated by practical circumstance and the condescending request of the then-celebrated Byron: "Timidly, as he tried to get some practical use out of what he had written earlier, he escorted it, as he was to escort so much by that time, with a cloud of apology." But 1816–17 was the period during which Coleridge wrote *The Statesman's Manual* and the *Lay Sermons*, some of his most pointed affirmations of vital, Christian philosophy over mechanistic Spinozan philosophy. He was also revising "The Eolian Harp" for inclusion in *Sibylline Leaves* (1817). Given the pious mood and substance of the works Coleridge produced during this time, it seems possible that the publication of "Kubla Khan" was strategic rather than accidental—that Coleridge sought to get some homiletic mileage out of what, for the 1798 poet, may have been heretical, nihilistic poetry. In the context of Coleridge's later works, the poem is no longer a transgression but an injunction against transgression; it is, in the language of the accompanying preface, the inverse yet "parallel production of the correspondent expressions" of Coleridge's mature prose. Both forewarn against the hazards of

Mammon-worship, the dangers of secular, counterfeit symbolism, and alienation from the organic, divine symbolism of scripture.

—Claire Miller Colombo, "Reading Scripture, Writing Self: Coleridge's Animation of the 'Dead Letter,'" *Studies in Romanticism* 35, no. 1 (Spring 1996): pp. 43–45.

KATHLEEN WHEELER ON THE POEM'S RELATION TO 18TH-CENTURY GARDEN CONCEPTS

[Kathleen Wheeler is a well-known critic and the author of several books on Romanticism, including *The Creative Mind in Coleridge's Poetry* (1981) and *Romanticism, Pragmatism and Deconstruction* (1993). In the excerpt below from her article "'Kubla Khan' and Eighteenth Century Aesthetic Theories," Wheeler discusses the poem within the context of that century's interest in gardens, most particularly the popular Chinese garden, and its significance to debates on the nature of artistic inspiration and mechanical versus organic concepts of nature.]

Few poems of classic status in the English literary corpus seem more exotic to the modern reader than "Kubla Khan." Coleridge's tantalising account of its origins combines with the Oriental imagery to tend to disassociate the poem from its literary tradition. The perhaps surprising conclusion persists however that if ever a poem reflected the concerns and interests of its age, "Kubla Khan" is that poem. Yet the works on sources has acted both to obscure and to reveal the exemplary nature of the poem. For it has located many coincidences of idea, imagery and phrase in travelogues, histories, religious myths, and Oriental literature generally, without emphasising sufficiently (to overcome the strangeness to a modern reader) the extent to which much of this material had already been assimilated into the English literary tradition in the eighteenth century, and already constituted exciting and well-known speculations of the day.

Johnson's *Rasselas* is a work which helps to indicate how commonplace and familiar in English literature Oriental imagery, with its earthly paradises and exotic guests had become. Published in 1759, *Rasselas* won immediate success in the contemporary climate of *Persian Tales* and *Arabian Nights.* Goldsmith's *Citizen of the World* (1762) is another of the most obvious and important cases, in spite of its critical, satiric mode, as is Beckford's *Vathek* (1786) which Byron was later to praise unrestrainedly and draw upon extensively. It is also clear that Coleridge unequivocally rejected the moralising "improvements" to the Oriental tale of Addison, Steele, Johnson, Hawkesworth, and Ridley, and he probably would have also have felt the pseudophilosophizing spirit of *Rasselas* and Voltaire's *Zadig* (1749) to be at cross purposes with the Oriental Tale. On the other hand, he would have sympathised with the satires of Walpole and Goldsmith on the author-translators of the numerous pseudo-tales.

For Coleridge's own adept use of prefaces (and glosses) mimics often ironically the technique of authors' and translators' prefaces of many of the collections of Oriental Tales or English adaptations; he also realised how effective these techniques were in intensifying poetic illusion by projecting the origin and authorship of the tale into some distant and unknown time and country, or into some unusual state of mind. He wove a framework technique into the verse structure of his own poems, either explicitly as in "The Ancient Mariner," or in the form of a radical change in the narrative perspective, as in stanza iv of "Kubla Khan," thus imitating the Chinese-box structure of many tales. He thereby drew attention to the role of the story-teller in both poems, as was done so effectively in *Arabian Nights.* He also often made unity of apparently disconnected images an explicit issue, as in the preface to "Kubla Khan." And he preserved the action of the poems well outside the realm of reality or possibility (as he ironically owned to Mrs. Barbauld). This Coleridgean kind of supernaturalism became moreover the direct mode of displaying imaginative symbol-making, or what we call "figuration" (the production of figures of speech) at its most universally representative, that is, in its form most free from any dogmatic or didactic purposes and consequently effective for instruction in the way appropriate to art, that is by means of delight. Finally, as will be discussed below, Coleridge showed how exotic and even extravagant imagery could be used in the service of that "educt of the imagination," the symbol, in order to direct the mind, first, towards the idea and the intelligential in and through the use of the sensuous, and, second, towards a self-consciousness about the mind's own processes and nature, which for Coleridge always constituted the genuine *unity* of a work of art.

The exploration of such a "unifying idea" as self-conscious awareness of the importance of figuration, toward which the imagery of "Kubla Khan" leads, can also be considered in the light of the less literary and more theoretical background of the aesthetic controversies raging in the eighteenth century. Dryden, Pope, Locke, Edmund Burke, John Baillie, Johnson and others contributed to the issues which were hotly debated, such as the relative value of painting and poetry, the nature of the sublime, the distinction between copy and imitation, the nature of genius, the analysis of language as literal or inherently metaphorical, and the role of rhetoric and emotion in poetry. This more theoretical direction is best approached by means of a brief excursus into the image of the garden in its eighteenth century context.

In addition to reflecting the interest in travels, foreign (and especially Oriental) cultures, fantastic speculations about the Nile, the cosmos, origins of man, the first language, and mysterious eastern cults of wisdom and religion (all of which were topics popular throughout the late seventeenth and eighteenth centuries), "Kubla Khan" also explicitly reflects the widespread interest in gardens, and particularly the oriental or "Chinese Garden" whose design was actually imported into the grounds of stately homes throughout England. However strange it may seem to the modern reader or poet, gardening was a subject worthy of discourses and poems by the most eminent writers, and was eagerly read about by an interested reading public. ⟨...⟩

The movement of "Kubla Khan" from the formal geometric garden of the seventeenth century to the suggestions of a more natural garden towards the end of stanza i ("forests ancient as the hills," and so on), and finally towards the wild and natural scene of stanza ii, seems to chart this gradual change in interest throughout the previous century and a half. It had of course its symbolic counterpart in the eighteenth century dispute of the nature of genius as dominated by a reasoning, measuring, analytical faculty or, alternatively, guided by a faculty of intuition, which was mysterious and acted according to its own, unknown, internal principles. Thus the garden symbol had its application in a theory of aesthetics as well as in a religious or moral sphere. Artifice was set up against inspiration, conscious against unconscious, and the mechanical against the organic. It was perhaps in the light of these eighteenth century controversies that Wordsworth formulated his theory of a return to natural feeling and the language of the common man.

—Kathleen Wheeler, "'Kubla Khan' and Eighteenth Century Aesthetic Theories," *The Wordsworth Circle* 22, no. 1 (Winter 1991): pp. 15, 16.

Works by
Samuel Taylor Coleridge

Lectures on Politics and Religion. 1795.

The Watchman. 1796.

Religious Musings. 1796.

Osorio. 1797.

Lyrical Ballads (with William Wordsworth). 1798. (second edition, 1800)

Wallenstein, a translation of Schiller. 1799–1800.

The Friend: A Series of Essays to Aid in the Formation of Fixed Principles in Politics, Morals and Religion. With Literary Amusements Interspersed. 1809–1810.

Remorse: A Tragedy in Five Acts. 1813.

Statesman's Manual. 1816.

Biographia Literaria, or Biographical Sketches of My Literary Life and Opinions. 1817

The Philosophical Lectures. 1818–1819.

Lay Sermons. 1825.

Aids to Reflection. 1825.

Seven Lectures on Shakespeare and Milton. 1829.

On the Constitution of Church and State. 1829

Specimens of the Table Talk of Samuel Taylor Coleridge (a collection of private conversations recorded by his nephew and literary executor, Henry N. Coleridge). 1835.

The Complete Works of Samuel Taylor Coleridge. 1871–1878.

Collected Letters of Samuel Taylor Coleridge. 1970.

Inquiring Spirit: A New Presentation of Coleridge from His Published and Unpublished Prose Writings. 1979.

The Notebooks of Samuel Taylor Coleridge, 3 volumes, 1794–1826.

Works About
Samuel Taylor Coleridge

Adair, Patricia M. *The Waking Dream: A Study of Coleridge's Poetry.* London: Edward Arnold, 1967.

Barth, J. Robert. *Coleridge and the Power of Love.* Columbia: University of Missouri Press, 1988.

Bate, Walter Jackson. *Coleridge.* New York: Macmillan, 1968.

Beer, John B. *Coleridge's Poetic Intelligence.* New York: Barnes & Noble Books, 1977.

Bloom, Harold, ed. *Romanticism and Consciousness: Essays in Criticism.* New York: W. W. Norton, 1970.

Bodkin, Maud. *Archetypal Patterns in Poetry: Psychological Studies of Imagination.* London: Oxford University Press, 1934.

Boulger, James. *Coleridge as Religious Thinker.* New Haven: Yale University Press, 1961.

Bygrave, Stephen. *Samuel Taylor Coleridge.* Plymouth, England: Northcote House, 1997.

Christensen, Jerome. *Coleridge's Blessed Machine of Language.* Ithaca, N.Y.: Cornell University Press, 1981.

Coburn, Kathleen. *Coleridge: A Collection of Critical Essays.* Englewood Cliffs, N.J.: Prentice-Hall, 1967.

Dekker, George. *Coleridge and the Literature of Sensibility.* New York: Barnes & Noble Books, 1978.

Fields, Beverly. *Reality's Dark Dream: Dejection in Coleridge.* Kent, Ohio: Kent State University Press, 1967.

Ford, Jennifer. *Coleridge on Dreaming: Romanticism, Dreams and the Medical Imagination.* New York: Cambridge University Press, 1998.

Fruman, Norman. *Coleridge: The Damaged Archangel.* New York: G. Braziller, 1971.

Fulford, Tim. *Coleridge's Figurative Language.* New York: St. Martin's Press, 1991.

Gallant, Christine. *Coleridge's Theory of Imagination Today.* New York: AMS Press, 1989.

Gravil, Richard, Lucy Newlyn, and Nicholas Roe, eds. *Coleridge's Imagination: Essays in Memory of Peter Laver.* New York: Cambridge University Press, 1985.

Hamilton, Paul. *Coleridge's Poetics.* Stanford, Calif.: Stanford University Press, 1983.

Harding, Anthony J. *Coleridge and the Idea of Love: Aspects of Relationship in Coleridge's Thought and Writing.* London, New York: Cambridge University Press, 1974.

———. *Coleridge and the Inspired Word.* Kingston, Ontario: McGill-Queen's University Press, 1985.

Hill, John Spencer. *A Coleridge Companion: An Introduction to the Major Poems.* New York: Macmillan, 1984.

Hodgson, John A. *Coleridge, Shelley and Transcendental Inquiry: Rhetoric, Argument, Metapsychology.* Lincoln: University of Nebraska Press, 1989.

Holmes, Richard. *Coleridge: Early Visions.* New York: Viking, 1990.

———. *Coleridge: Darker Reflections.* London: Harper Collins, 1998.

Keane, Patrick J. *Coleridge's Submerged Politics: The Ancient Mariner and Robinson Crusoe.* Columbia: University of Missouri Press, 1994.

Kearns, Sheila M. *Coleridge, Wordsworth and Romantic Biography: Reading Strategies of Self-Representation.* Madison, N.J.: Fairleigh Dickinson University Press, 1995.

Kessler, Edward. *Coleridge's Metaphors of Being.* Princeton, N.J.: Princeton University Press, 1979.

Lefebure, Molly. *Samuel Taylor Coleridge: A Bondage of Opium.* London: Gollancz, 1974.

Lockridge, Laurence. *Coleridge the Moralist.* Ithaca, N.Y.: Cornell University Press, 1977.

Magnuson, Paul. *Coleridge and Wordsworth: A Lyrical Dialogue.* Princeton, N.J.: Princeton University Press, 1988.

Marks, Emerson R. *Coleridge on the Language of Verse.* Princeton, N.J.: Princeton University Press, 1981.

Modiano, Raimonda. *Coleridge and the Concept of Nature.* Tallahassee: Florida State University Press, 1985.

Newlyn, Lucy. *Coleridge, Wordsworth and the Language of Allusion.* New York: Oxford University Press, 1986.

Paley, Morton D. *Coleridge's Later Poetry.* Oxford: Clarendon Press, 1996.

Parker, Reeve. *Coleridge's Meditative Art.* Ithaca, N.Y.: Cornell University Press, 1975.

Prickett, Stephen. *Coleridge and Wordsworth: The Poetry of Growth.* Cambridge: Cambridge University Press, 1970.

Rookmaaker, H. R. *Towards a Romantic Conception of Nature: Coleridge's Poetry Up to 1903, a Study in the History of Ideas.* Philadelphia: John Benjamins, 1984.

Simpson, David. *Irony and Authority in Romantic Poetry.* London: Macmillan, 1979.

Stillinger, Jack. *Coleridge and Textual Instability: The Multiple Versions of the Major Poems.* New York: Oxford University Press, 1994.

Taylor, Anya. *Coleridge's Defense of the Human.* Columbus: Ohio State University Press, 1986.

Walsh, William. *Coleridge: The Work and the Relevance.* London: Chatto & Windus, 1967.

Wheeler, Kathleen M. *The Creative Mind in Coleridge's Poetry.* Cambridge: Harvard University Press, 1981.

Index of
Themes and Ideas